Your Unique Career Path

Discover the Work that Works for You

Armen Alexanian

Copyright © 2017- Armen Alexanian

All rights reserved.

This book, or parts thereof, may not be reproduced in any form without the written permission from the author; exceptions are made for brief excerpts used in publication reviews.

Printed in the United States of America

ISBN-10: 0997620412

ISBN-13: 978-0997620412

10 9 8 7 6 5 4 3 2

Empire Publishing

www.empirebookpublishing.com

If you like the cover art or the artwork in the book, you can purchase it at: https://youruniquecareerpath.threadless.com/

Dedication

To my wife Amy, for making this possible.

To my boys. I hope these ideas help you go places where the streets are not marked.

To my parents, for your continuing love and support.

In memory of Roman Meshon, for showing me what mastery, joy, and work look like together.

Contents

Introduction 1

Chapter 1 Money Is Not What You Really Want 5
    Money Is No Object 7
    Money Shouldn't Determine Your Career 10
    Using Money Efficiently 13
    What You Do Really Want 18
    Chapter 1 Exercises 21

Chapter 2 Achievement Clarified 25
    Measuring Achievement 25
    Your Higher Goal 28
    Failure Is a Weasel Word 30
    Chapter 2 Exercises 32

Chapter 3 Education 35
    Redshirting 37
    College is a Time, Not a Place 39
    Creating Options for Yourself 41
    Synergistic Disciplines 43
    Chapter 3 Exercises 45

Chapter 4 Self Confidence 49
    Your Unique Personal Mojo 51
    Confidence Success Multiplier 53
    Attitude, Not Aptitude 58
    Personal Pacing 61
    Chapter 4 Exercises 64

Chapter 5 Personal Inventory 67
    Health 69
    Attitude 75

    Finances 77
    Relationships 79
    Decisions 81
    Chapter 5 Exercises 84
Chapter 6 **Identify Your Interests** 87
    How Do You Know If Something Is Right for You? 88
    The Chicken or the Egg 92
    Four-Step Work Identification Process 95
    Day of Kindness 98
    Chapter 6 Exercises 100
Chapter 7 **Take Your Work Seriously** 103
    Doing Your Duty 106
    Professional Portfolio 108
    Goal Setting 110
    Chapter 7 Exercises 113
Conclusion 115
Career Principles 117
Contributor Acknowledgement 118

Introduction

Would you quit your job today if I gave you $10 million? If so, this book is for you. If not, you can put this book down because you probably don't need it.

Many books have been written to help readers choose a career. They feature personality and skill tests which are designed to narrow the options and match people with a suitable choice. While well-intentioned, these methods approach the process backwards. They're based on the idea that each career has a specific set of attributes and that each person has specific skills and personality and that it's just a matter of matching the person to a career. The notion that your best skills should determine what you should do for your career is arbitrarily limiting, disrespects your true multi-dimensional nature, and underestimates your ability to learn and grow. In the same way that judging someone based on his or her physical appearance is unfair, limiting your options based on your current skills, interests or performance level is also misguided.

The purpose of this book is not to help you choose a career. Rather, it is to teach you new ways to think about the questions and challenges you will face on your career journey. This book upends traditional notions you may have been taught about careers and arms you with new perspectives. It reframes the problem of career choice in ways that make your thought process easier and the action steps you should take more obvious.

Much of what we've been taught about lifelong work is based on the outdated paradigm of choosing a specific career and riding it to success. The process is essentially an exercise in attempting to imagine yourself in some predefined roles, choosing one, and then trying to mold yourself into that specific identity and set of behaviors. The very act of choosing an option already defined by someone else takes away your creative power to design a career that resonates with your highest values and interests. This causes career seekers to spend the majority of their effort looking for external opportunities rather than discovering their skills and defining for themselves how they will provide value to others.

This book is titled "Your Unique Career Path" because your vocation should not be something predefined by someone else, like an entrée that you choose from a restaurant menu. There doesn't need to be a named profession falling into some predefined category for you to be able to produce value for other people. With the fast pace of modern technology and human progress, it makes more sense to focus on yourself and how you can add value in this new environment than on some predefined, prenamed career. You're a unique person. There's no reason to believe your career won't be as unique as you are.

The key reason most people don't find fulfilling careers is ignorance - of themselves and of the external world. Every person has an abundance of innate talents, abilities and curiosity to fill one hundred productive lifetimes. Sadly, few people realize their incredible potential because it takes time and work to uncover and develop it. Many have the false belief that they already know themselves well enough to make good decisions about their careers. They also falsely believe they have a good understanding of what is available to them. An enormous amount of exciting development is happening around the world in every area you can imagine, and even more so in areas you've never imagined. Traditional university training only scratches the surface in terms of exploring students' potential, giving them valuable skills, and exposing them to all that's available. True career exploration begins through personal exposure to as many interesting areas as possible and by trying as many new things as possible.

Under this paradigm, the daunting task of choosing a career is reduced to the much easier questions of, "What skills can I learn right now?", "What types of exposure are available?" and "What can I add to my portfolio which will broaden what I can offer to others?" If at any point you feel unsure about what work to do, it means you need to have more experiences, gain more useful skills, and learn more about yourself and your community. The better you develop yourself and understand what's going on in the world, the more value you'll be able to exchange through your professional pursuits. As your interests change over time and you evolve as a person, it's only natural that what you choose to do for work will also evolve. This book is intended as a guide to help you become the kind of person who has many enticing options to choose from and for whom deciding among these options is straightforward and personally fulfilling.

Each chapter in this book presents a central principle supported by fresh perspectives. This is an action-oriented book. Each chapter is followed by exercises to complete. Some are introspective, some encourage you to work with other people, and some require you to go out and have certain experiences and evaluate your feelings afterwards. The exercises are meant for you to get to know yourself better and to serve as a starting point in your career exploration. You'll get out of this book what you put into it. So, your responses to the questions, the material you gather during the exercises, and your unique experiences and reactions will serve as your starting point for building your career.

After reading this book, your thought process should be clearer, making the next steps in your career more obvious. Be warned however, if you do this right, your journey will be longer and more challenging. If you're looking for easy answers, I suggest you put down this book and walk away because it doesn't contain any. The road I'm offering you is long, bumpy, exhausting, and often difficult. The easier road my competition is offering is paved with good intentions.

Are you ready to get started?

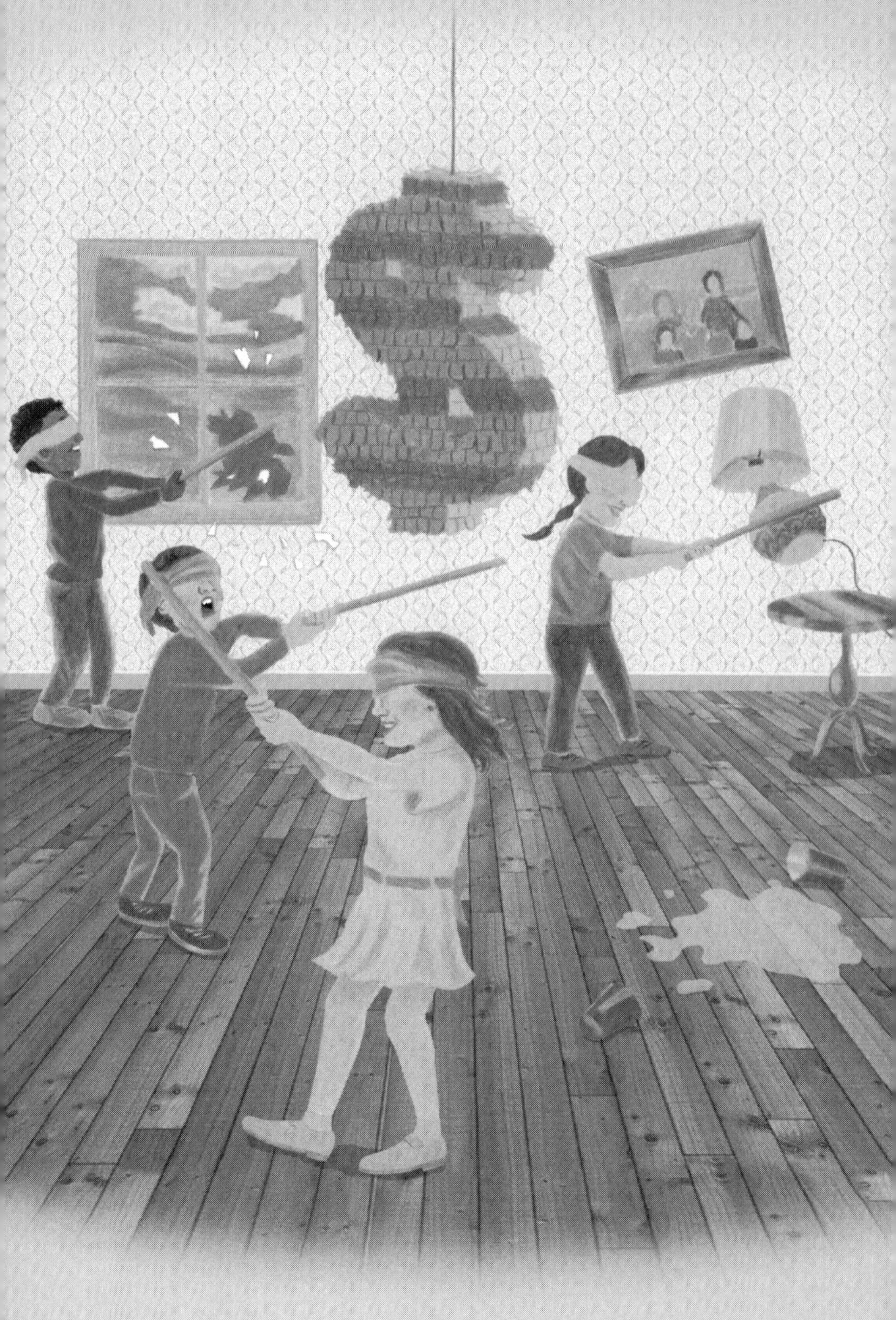

Chapter 1

Money Is Not What You Really Want

I started reading motivational books as a teenager, hoping they would help me discover what to do with my life. Too many of these books assumed that my goal was wealth and went about explaining how to get it. Famous books with the words "rich", "millionaire", and "wealthy" in the titles made me feel inadequate because I hadn't amassed any wealth and wasn't sure how to go about it. The books instructed readers to evaluate their career interests with the litmus test of whether they would "create wealth" under the presumption that wealth carries with it some moral authority.

The financial crisis of 2008 showed us how easy it is to let the pursuit of wealth usurp our values. Later, we'll discuss how to engage your values in managing your career and finances. Rather than focus on "being rich" (whatever that means), you should define and pursue a specific outcome you desire in your life. You will employ and manage many resources, including money, as tools to produce that outcome. The specific outcome is your goal and money is but one of your tools, not the other way around.

Do you know what would truly make you happy? Many people, if asked what they really want, would say they want to be rich. Do you know exactly what you would do if you had all the money you wanted? To what degree does lack of money actually hold anyone back from something they really want? It only holds people back who only want money! Because money is such an important and often controversial topic, it's essential to begin this exploration of your focus by dispelling the idea that the answer might be money.

Those who wish to become rich for its own sake want to be full-time consumers. That is, not having to bother with producing anything. The main reason most people want lots of money is so they don't have to work for a living. Yet, many don't realize that their desire not to work is the very reason they do still have to work and don't have enough money to retire. This is because wealth is defined as the amount you produce in excess of what you consume. Someone who doesn't produce much more than he or she consumes will never accumulate wealth. Therefore, those who don't want to work will always have to! Lack of personal drive and industry goes hand in hand with being bankrupt financially and emotionally. If you'll notice, many people who have enough money to retire don't actually stop working. They keep doing either what made them wealthy or other productive things with their lives.

One of two things happens when someone becomes a consumer and stops producing. He either consumes too quickly and runs out of money, or he reaches a point where he gets bored with consuming and becomes dissatisfied. If he has a healthy outlook, he'll start to wonder what else life has to offer. If he has an unhealthy outlook, he may pursue drugs or risky experiences. If all someone does is consume and engage in leisure activities, he soon realizes his life has little meaning or value. The optimal condition for human beings is to be healthy, happy, productive, and supportive of each other. You derive real meaning in your life only to the degree that you add value to the lives of others. The purpose of this chapter is to emphasize the principle that you should *make your career goal something specific other than money.*

Money Is No Object

While studying business in college, I learned the term fungible. It's a funny-sounding word which describes things which are perfectly interchangeable or homogenous. For example, barrels of crude oil, ounces of gold, pieces of macaroni from a box of pasta, and store-bought dinner rolls are fungible. Each individual one is exactly like the others in terms of its value, form, and function. Money, whether in the form of physical currency or bank balances, is fungible. Your money is just as good as my money. If you're buying something at a store, they don't care if you pay with ten-dollar bills or twenty-dollar bills and they don't care if you pay for the items you choose or if I buy them for you. It's all the same to the store owner as long as the money is received in a form in which it can be processed.

Money eludes most people because they view it as a specific object in and of itself. Money is never an end; it's always only an indirect result. It's not like exercise where the more you do, the stronger you get, or studying where the more you study, the more you learn. It's impossible to make money your specific goal because of its fungible, non-specific nature. Trying to make money into a goal is like trying to hug a ghost, it's impossible! Money is only made as a result of doing something of value for others. There are only two groups of people for whom money is an end result: thieves who take other people's money without providing value, and the Bureau of Engraving and Printing which actually manufactures money. In order to make something happen in your life, you need to identify that something specifically. Money cannot be your something because it only comes about as an indirect result of your actions.

You need to earn enough money to pay your expenses, save for retirement, and live a comfortable lifestyle. However, don't make the mistake of letting your need for money become your drive or your goal. Trying to make money an end in itself leads to unsatisfying and often unsavory paths. This is because you're trying to skip the part where you deliver value to others. The spirit of wealth-creation makes delivering value to others the end goal. From the perspective of the parties in a transaction, each receives something of greater value than what they gave. The wealth is the excess perceived value received on both sides. Attempting to circumvent this process places undeserved emphasis on bank balances rather than on the quality and value of the product or service you're offering.

If you ask yourself how you can provide the most value for others, you begin down the path of introspection, self-improvement, and helping others on as big a scale as possible. This will likely have financial rewards for you and will certainly result in great intangible benefits from serving others. If you're asking yourself why you haven't made very much money, the answer lies in how much value you've delivered to others. In general, the people who provide the most value possible to the largest number of people reap the most financial rewards. Hundreds of millions of people use Microsoft software and Microsoft is very wealthy. Tens of millions of people enjoy watching televised sports events and the players make a lot of money. The same is true for popular musicians. You'll earn more money when you increase the value of what you do and the size of the audience that is benefiting.

Few people really want to be rich for its own sake, though many think they do. Being rich is equivalent to everything in the world that can be purchased with money being free for you. Sensible people don't actually want to be rich or even own extravagant possessions like fancy cars and mansions. All they really want is some kind of assurance that their present and future human needs will be met. I've read many articles which showcase famous peoples' homes for sale. Often, the celebrities haven't even lived in those homes for very long and are looking to sell. I imagine that the owners were initially excited that they could afford the fancy homes but the excitement wore off after a while because the home didn't actually resonate with what the owners really wanted out of life or reflect how they actually lived, day-to-day. It's likely they didn't spend enough time considering how they actually operated their lives and whether that house would maximize their efficiency and enjoyment. The opulent homes turned out to be just large, expensive, fancy buildings. The human ego, ever seeking to expand itself, clings to extravagance but is ultimately unfulfilled. The reason for this is that most of the trappings of being rich don't align with what people actually need in order to be fulfilled.

People focus too much on attaining money rather than on attaining something specific they actually want. Money is a distraction from what you are really looking for in life. Many don't realize this until they have a lot of money. I know several wealthy people whom I would not describe as truly happy because they focused on money rather than on the specific things in life that bring them joy. Stuck in this mindset, they believe that having even more money will finally lead to fulfillment. Focus more on the specific things you want and less on money. The more specifically you can define what you want, the closer you are to getting it.

Money is neither a barrier nor a vehicle to what you desire. Don't automatically assume that you need money in order to get what you want. It's like assuming you need money to make friends or to meet a romantic partner. It's a shallow, unenlightened notion. There are many ways to manifest what you want without having to first acquire money to get it. I like the phrase 'Money is no object'. It's true. Money is not the object; the object is the object! So what's your object?

Money Shouldn't Determine Your Career

Do you know how you can easily tell if you're in the wrong career? Just imagine how your life would change if you suddenly received $10 million. If you would immediately quit your job or end your current career, then you're definitely in the wrong career. Does your 'wealthy self' have a completely different lifestyle from your current self? If so, this is likely why you are not wealthy. Think about it. People who become wealthy don't suddenly stop doing what made them wealthy. Indeed, they continue doing more of it. If you're not happy with what you're doing now and you'd immediately quit your job if you could, it means you're not living the life you really want and you're not moving closer to any desired set of circumstances. It means you're not engaging your creative energies regularly towards a life you really desire. By striving for money rather than a specific set of goals, you're repelling rather than attracting what you really want. Most wealthy people work more than average, rather than less, because they're motivated by something greater than basic survival. They're trying to create something interesting or valuable for others which results in wealth creation. If your ideal wealthy self is just a consumer who stays home all day watching daytime TV, you'll probably never become wealthy with such feeble ambitions. If, however, your wealthy self is busy producing valuable goods or services for others, you're already on your way to becoming wealthy and your daily life won't change much when you get there. Is your 'wealthy self' holding you back?

Billionaire entrepreneurs appear in the news quite often, describing their latest ventures. You'd think they live lives of leisure, never lifting a finger, but quite the opposite is true. They're extremely busy people who use their time wisely because it is their greatest asset. Most of them work much harder than you do and enjoy it more. And they do this by choice. Are you working in your job purely by choice or because you have to make a living? Keep in mind that working by choice takes a lot of time and effort. However, you can identify what you really enjoy and start taking steps towards having a career that you would keep even if you were rich. You don't have to wait until you have a lot of money to start thinking and acting like your 'wealthy self'.

I once met someone who had made a few million dollars from stock options he had sold from having worked at an internet startup company. I asked him why he bothered to go to work every day and deal with the issues at another corporate job. He said he did "the whole not working thing" for two years during which he traveled and slept a lot. Afterward, he just got bored and felt like he wanted to do something productive. After traveling the world and taking fancy vacations, wealthy people still need to figure out how to spend their time every day, hopefully in creative and productive ways. The point is for you to attain this mindset at the beginning of your career without having to be wealthy first. Most people never progress to the stage where they are faced with this question because they're too busy supporting themselves financially.

You don't have to wait until you're wealthy to decide what you would do if you were. As much as is feasible, you should design your lifestyle as it would be if you didn't have to work full time. I don't mean that you should suddenly go out and buy expensive toys or go on expensive vacations. Instead, you should thoughtfully consider how you would use your time on a daily basis. This includes which projects you would work on, which people you would associate with, and how you would develop yourself and help others. That way, when you do gain more success, your lifestyle won't necessarily change. You'll already be poised to fine-tune the brute force of your new wealth to continue what you were already doing.

I once interviewed a busy architect about what he would do if he had enough money that he didn't have to work. He told me that he'd keep his same job but just renegotiate his weekly schedule with his employer so it was more convenient. He wanted to continue the same work as before, just doing so on his own terms. That's my definition of success.

A friend of mine in San Francisco sometimes reads news articles about successful Internet entrepreneurs who've sold their businesses for millions of dollars and asks me why I'm not trying to do something similar. This has the effect of devaluing what I am doing because I'm making less money than the people in those articles. Does that mean that I should stop what I'm doing and try to replicate their success in the hope of making more money? I work in my field because I'm good at it and I enjoy it. Money should come as a result of doing what brings joy to you and value to others. When people make money their main emphasis, they take their focus off providing the most value possible for others, and the quality of their work and offerings declines. However, when you're motivated by joy, the steps you take toward your goal won't feel like drudgery but will instead be fueled by a sense of purpose and inspiration. You will feel as though you're birthing something new into the world. It will feel less like work and more like passion. I know this because this is how I feel now as I write these words at 2:30 am!

It makes no sense to work at an unfulfilling job just to make money so you can arrange your life for happiness during the hours of the week when you're not at work. Instead, find a career that stimulates you. When you enjoy your weekdays, and your creativity is being stretched and challenged, you will excel in your work and reap the benefits. It's essential that you are energized and engaged in your work. When you're not, it's a waste of your time and your employer's money. Remember, when it concerns your relationships, you should follow your heart. When it concerns your career, you should follow your art!

Using Money Efficiently

Money represents the ability to use brute force to perform a task or acquire something. Let's say you just bought a heavy, new refrigerator and it was delivered outside your house while you were away and now you need to move it into the kitchen. You could use the brute force of money to hire some people to put it in the right spot. However, there are other clever ways you can achieve this by yourself without using brute force. You could borrow your neighbor's dolly to wheel the refrigerator in and he or she might help you. You could use the packaging materials that came with the refrigerator to create a ramp to push it up the door landing. You could also use the cardboard box as a platform to slide the fridge across the floor. There are countless other creative ways to get the fridge to the spot you need it that don't require spending any money.

Saying you want lots of money is equivalent to saying you want lots of brute force. But to what end? Money is not an end in itself. It's a force, that if used carefully, can arrange human life in a way that sets the stage for happiness. I've worked for many companies that have spent a lot of money, sometimes in vain, to achieve a specific result. I've learned that in many cases, the money alone wasn't sufficient. I watched them waste lots of money without achieving their goals. Because the money involved wasn't the corporate executives' personal money, they applied it recklessly without high-quality thought and without a prudent plan. Conversely, having much less money to spend would have forced them to think more creatively and spend each dollar more judiciously.

When you get a new tube of toothpaste, you often use much more than you need the first several times because there's so much contained in the full tube. But when you get down to the very end, you squeeze with all your might to get that last little bit out of the tube. The first several servings of toothpaste mostly go to waste. If you start by using a small amount each time, it lasts much longer. Here's a pro tip. When you can't squeeze any more toothpaste out of the tube, cut the tube with a scissors and you'll find there's at least a week's worth of extra toothpaste in there. That advice alone is worth the price of this book!

The same is true with money. People who have access to a lot of money tend to use less care and creativity in spending than they would if they had much less money to spend. There are many life-hacker strategies for achieving a lot with a small amount of money. The amount of money you have available now doesn't prevent you from starting almost any project you can think of. Most businesses can be launched at a very small scale and ramped up in relation to their profitability and the owner's enthusiasm.

If you focus on getting money, you haven't increased your specificity or narrowed your goal at all. However, if you focus your energy on a specific goal, you'll find ways to minimize the amount of money needed to achieve it. The more specifically you define it, the closer you are to achieving it. The very first step to getting there is for you to imagine the world as if you already have it. If you demonstrate to those around you a high level of commitment, they're likely to help you find ways to finance it. To drive profitability and financial success you need to maximize the efficiency and value of the specific activity you are performing.

Wealthy people face the question of how to spend their time from day to day from a different perspective - that of having more options than most people. This is one of those 'nice problems to have' but what makes it interesting is what the answers they choose tell us about their relationship with money. Well-adjusted folks tend to remain wealthy while maladapted ones usually lose their money. Many people have latent personal psychological issues which remain hidden by their financial limitations. These issues get infrequent exposure due to time limitations imposed by full-time work. When such a person comes into wealth, these issues manifest because he is left to his own now more potent and often chaotic devices which can spiral out of control. I recently watched a fascinating documentary which detailed the stories of people who suddenly came into tremendous wealth. They squandered millions of dollars in a short time because of their unfortunate orientation towards money. The excitement of wielding monetary power combined with ignorance of personal finance concepts led them to spend it in unwise ways and end up not only losing the money but also going into debt in many cases.

People who have difficulty with money misunderstand its nature. Their primary understanding of it is as a force that provides immediate fulfillment and status through the acquisition of material goods. They're unable to take pleasure in the banal realities of their everyday lives and they see money as a path to happiness. People who suddenly come into lots of money are often surprised to find that it doesn't make them happy after the initial elation wears off. Happiness comes from your ability to derive pleasure from your current circumstances and use them as a springboard to do even more interesting things. When you truly appreciate what you already have, it creates an attitude that allows you to see the magic infused in even the most mundane things. Money can't buy you this attitude; it can only distract you from it. Money doesn't make you better, smarter or more interesting. It just gives you more brute force.

The best reason to desire money is "so that", not for its own sake. You should want money "so that" you can fulfill your basic needs, "so that" you can start a business, "so that" you can purchase woodworking equipment or add a garage to your house, or buy plane tickets to France. Money should help facilitate things or experiences you want to create. Your desired things and experiences are your object, not the money itself. To provoke thought about the best uses of money, I present my "money value hierarchy" below which ranks and describes various ways of using money.

Money Value Hierarchy

1. Fulfill basic human needs.

The best use for money is to provide for people's most basic immediate needs including food, clothing, shelter, and anything essential to the maintenance of human life and safety.

2. Ameliorate negative circumstances.

Money is extremely useful in helping sick or injured people get well, fixing things that are broken, helping needy people, and improving circumstances. For example, the kitchen in my house had not been redone since the 1970s and was in terrible shape. Counter and floor tiles were broken, the sink was leaky, shelves and drawers were broken and rotting and the eating area only provided seating for two people. It was a tremendous relief to finally renovate the kitchen and improve every aspect of its layout and function. It's now much more convenient and fits my family's needs. However, at this point, more space, appliances, cabinets, lights, or decorations would not add any more value. Now that the kitchen meets a satisfactory standard, spending more money would yield no incremental value.

One of the most important circumstances that money can ameliorate is the need to provide for the elderly. Everyone should save and invest money for their retirement in order to provide for themselves when they are no longer able to work. When it comes to saving money, the earlier the better!

3. Build, create, and facilitate.

Money can build homes, factories, cars, computers, businesses and all the physical artifacts of modern human life. To the degree that a person, family, organization or society can benefit from these, money can add enormous value by allowing people to manage their lives and work more efficiently. It can also create opportunities for people to meet, form new relationships, and have new experiences. By 2004 I had saved enough money to spend three months living with a family and studying French with my wife in Lyon, France. I learned a lot, improved my French, made some good friends, and had a great time. Many philanthropists derive great value from providing scholarships for students, building homes in poor regions, and helping entrepreneurs everywhere create sustainable businesses.

4. Choose whether or not to work.

The most profound way money can change your life beyond meeting your basic needs is giving you the choice of whether or not to work. If you must work for a living, the largest part of your time and energy is spent working. Most people don't mind working itself but harbor an existential angst against the necessity of having to work in order to survive. The activities you would do if you didn't have to work should inform your approach to your current work. You should strive to build your career such that the work you're doing is what you would otherwise choose if you were totally financially independent.

5. Rent luxuries.

It's true that rich people have nice toys. These luxuries typically provide a short term feeling of elation. The mansions of rich and famous people I've seen look less like cozy homes and more like fancy hotels. Even the fanciest car becomes humdrum within a few months. There's a reason why most fancy material goods depreciate so quickly - they yield low value in relation to their cost. You can drive across town in a $10,000 used Honda just as easily as you can in a $200,000 Ferrari. Companies that produce and sell luxury items earn tremendous profits by taking advantage of people's egocentric desire to feel important and impress others. I recommend experiencing luxury items once in a while for the fun of it as well as to dispel the mystery. The best way to do so is by renting! You can rent fancy cars, clothes, jet skis, boats, and even ski lodges. By renting these things you experience the excitement they provide while acknowledging the short-term, illusory nature of their value.

What You Do Really Want

What people really want, beyond the satisfaction of their basic needs and comforts, is intangible. We all want essentially the same things: freedom, excitement, love, companionship, knowledge, wisdom, and expertise. We want good health, vibrancy, humor, leadership, kindness, achievement, self-expression, creativity, and the thrill that comes from overcoming challenges. What differentiates people is the way in which they experience these intangibles. This means that the question: "What do you want?" is actually misleading because it points you in the direction of tangible answers or answers outside yourself, like money, a job, a house, a car or a relationship. How often have you wanted something, finally gotten it, and found out that it didn't make you feel the way you thought it would? The value of material things in our lives quickly reaches the point of diminishing returns. A delicious meal at a nice restaurant is wonderful but you couldn't eat three or four such meals in one sitting. And if you did you'd feel awful! Unless you have a huge family, or invite your friends over for indoor full-court basketball regularly, you're not going to enjoy a 20,000 square foot house. Once you find a home and neighborhood that fit your family well, more house doesn't yield more value for you. Rather than trying to get intangible feelings through tangible things, skip over the tangibles and head right for the intangibles straight away.

What you really want are these intangible feelings. The best way to mesh your values with your career pursuits is to determine specific ways to create these intangible feelings. The question you should be asking is, "How will I create these positive feelings and experiences in my life?" This points you in the direction of taking action and engages your values and creativity together. If you ask your mind what you really want, it will respond with some tangible thing. Such things, like a big house or a fancy car may take you a long time to get and once you do, they may not fulfill you for long. But by asking yourself how you can create a positive experience, your mind will look for creative answers that don't always involve tangible ownership. You and a friend could rent a Ferrari for the day and have an outrageous exciting time and then take it back. You will have experienced excitement without having to own the car. You could start a business helping other people experience thrills and excitement! You could prepare a dinner for a needy family and create feelings of kindness and love without having to be a wealthy philanthropist.

So now that I've identified a better question for you to ask yourself, I'm going to give you half of the answer up front. What a value this is! I'm giving you the question plus half of the answer! That's three fourths of the whole equation. You're almost there; now all you have to do is come up with the second half of the answer. So, we'll begin again with the question, "How will I create positive feelings and experiences in my life?" Now, here's the first half of your answer: you will create these feelings and experiences through other people.

You can't achieve what you want in life by yourself. You will create these positive feelings with and for other people. If you learn to make other people happy, it will make you happy. If you earn money for other people, you will earn money. If you make other people laugh, you will feel funny. Your answer should be specific in describing how you will achieve your goal. Examples of good answers include:

"I feel happy and humorous by performing stand-up comedy on Mondays at the comedy club."
"I experience vibrant health, strength, and excitement in my monthly swimming competitions."
"I gain the feeling of financial security by consulting with my graphic arts clients ."
"I feel compassion and love by volunteering at the animal shelter on Sunday afternoons."
"I feel satisfaction and fulfillment by working as a medical doctor in poor countries."
"I achieve freedom and financial independence for myself and others by helping people start small businesses."

If you have a project that's important to you, don't waste any time worrying about how it will turn out. Let your enthusiasm be your only guide. If you think something is interesting or valuable, that's all that matters. If it doesn't catch on with other people, it's still a project you completed that can have ongoing value in some way. Do it for yourself because you like it. If you develop something useful that you enjoy that employs your best creative spirit, that's a tremendous success that may yield unforeseen future benefits.

Contrast the feelings described above with the idea of doing something just for the money. When you're doing something just for money, you tend to compromise and cut corners. Find a pursuit you want to do for its own sake - your own personal project or a business that you and a few close friends develop. Here's a way to practically guarantee success: find something you enjoy doing so much that someone would have to pay you not to do it! You would have to pay me a million dollars to permanently stop talking with people about their careers. And even then I may not be able to do it. If you like something that much, it won't matter if it's not a big success right away because you're doing it for the right reasons. Over time, as you develop your idea and its value proposition, it will evolve into something of lasting benefit to you and others.

Chapter 1 Exercises

Exercise 1. Millionaire

Get three sheets of paper and on the top of each one write $1 Million, $10 Million, and $100 Million. On the first sheet, write a list of exactly what you would do with $1 million. Include which debts you'd pay off, what things you'd buy for yourself and others, what vacations you would take, how much you would save, and how you would live your daily life. On the second and third sheets of paper, do the same, but for $10 million and $100 million. When I performed this exercise, I referenced everything from the first page and then included new things made possible by the extra money on the following pages. In what ways did the latter pages differ from the former ones? Examine how your life changes from page to page. What happens to your daily life once you become debt-free and no longer have to work for a living? How do you compare the value of the material things you can buy versus the freedom of not having to work every day? Of all the things you've written, are there any which motivate you to take action today?

A great way to do this is with a friend who can keep you focused and challenge your ideas. After both of you have completed the exercise, exchange your papers and critique your friend's items by challenging whether he or she would really need that much money in order to do or get each item on the list. You'll be surprised at how creative you can be in figuring out how to do the same thing with less money. Discuss what this means about what you can already experience and achieve right now in your current life. Where would money come in most handy and where is it mostly superfluous? Consider if it really is money that is holding you back or if it could be something completely different.

Exercise 2. Creating Positive Feelings

Write down at least five statements that follow this format: "I feel [insert feeling here] by doing [insert activity here] with/for [insert person or group of people here]." An example might be, "I feel proud when I teach new swim strokes to my students at the community pool." These can be things you currently experience or would like to experience in the future. Now ask yourself what it would take for you to have these experiences more often. Whom do you know that might be interested in participating? Don't tone down your statements based on what you think is "reasonable". Include as many outrageous items as you can, as long as they resonate with you. Consider ways you could incorporate each statement into your current life.

Exercise 3. Practice "Wasting" Money.

If you can accumulate some experiences "wasting" small amounts of money, it can be helpful when larger quantities are at stake because the feelings involved are essentially the same. If you have children, or are an aunt or uncle or have younger cousins, take several of them and their friends to a video game arcade. The more children, the better. You can get the feeling of being a "big spender" out of your system while at the same time examining your feelings of anxiety while the children spend the money as fast as you give it to them. Stay at the arcade for a full hour. Cash in enough money for quarters or tokens so that when you put them in your pockets, you get the feeling of being weighed down by all the heavy coins. Rather than divide all the tokens among the children, dispense them a few at a time to each child and watch how quickly they spend the tokens and return for more. Some games are designed to last for a few minutes while others are finished in seconds. Some of the games return tickets to the players which can be exchanged for candy or cheap toys later. This is designed to make the players feel they got some value in exchange for playing and encourage them to play more to get more tickets. This scheme is brilliant because the children never fail to get excited when they receive the tickets. Continue buying more tokens and giving them out as quickly as the children ask for them until the hour is complete. Make a note of how you feel each time you hand over some tokens and how quickly your pockets become lighter. How does it feel when you run out of tokens and have to get more cash out of your wallet to buy more? How much money did you end up spending during the hour? It goes very quickly! Now that you've "wasted" a bunch of money, remember the uncomfortable feelings you had and use them to help you spend money more prudently in the future.

Chapter 2

Achievement Clarified

Throughout childhood and beyond, you were taught the value of "achievement" from various sources. Parents, family members, and teachers tried to convince you that you had a responsibility to achieve a number of things, in a specified time, and that you'd better start working on them right away, lest you fall behind. Your mentors expected you to achieve things in the areas of academics, sports, extracurricular activities, and whatever other areas they felt would satisfy them about your performance. All these areas of achievement had long since been calibrated with well-established measurement systems capable of immediately sizing you up the moment you began. Before you knew it, you were measured, evaluated, ranked, categorized and judged based on criteria which you took no part in creating and over which you had no control. These people, though usually well-intentioned, compelled you to accept their specific paradigms of achievement before you had the chance to evaluate them for yourself. In this chapter, I present a new paradigm of achievement that you may accept or reject on your own terms: *Measure your achievement based solely on the amount of value you provide for other people.*

Measuring Achievement

In pretty much all areas of human endeavor, real achievement should be measured based on how much value a person or group brings to humanity as a whole. Getting straight A's, a PhD, an MD degree, a high-paying job, or valuable stock options are only real achievements to the degree that they end up benefiting other people. If you want to become a doctor and start helping sick people, you're required to get an MD degree. But the degree itself isn't the achievement; it's the quantifiable benefit you deliver to the patients. Winning competitive events like a professional sports championship, or the Olympic games is only an achievement to the degree that you've entertained or inspired people, not because you won the game or scored the most points. Athletes who compete with heart and act with grace and dignity on and off the court achieve tremendous value by serving as good role models for young people, not simply by defeating their opponents. There's a fine line between playing a sport because of the joy and thrill of the competition, and the desire to win for the sake of winning. Apart from its entertainment value and the fact that professional sports employ many people, a team winning a major professional sports competition is no more of an achievement than beating your friend in a game of beer pong!

The same is true for being declared "the best" at anything. If you're declared the best stand-up comedian because your jokes made people laugh and enjoy themselves, that's an achievement because you made them feel good, reduced their stress, and helped them relax. If you won a barbecue sauce contest because the deliciousness of your sauce delivered pleasure to many people, then that's also an achievement. However, most of the time, the pursuit of being the best at something comes from an ego-based need to fulfill some psychological yearning. A more worthwhile goal is delivering as much value possible to as many people as possible. For example, if you design a software application that improves the lives of many people, or if you figure out a way to deliver a thousand Christmas dinners to struggling families, those are incredible achievements because they benefited others.

Pay closer attention the next time you hear someone say he wants to be the best at some activity. Ask yourself, "What for?" and "How does that person being judged the best help people more than if someone else were declared the best?" Consider how silly and self-centered it sounds to want to be the best. What's the point of comparing yourself to other people? If you happen to be the best, good for you! But don't consider it an achievement; consider it more of a temporary status you can use to help other people improve. Don't feel bad if you're not the best at something. The concept of being the best is, at best, nonsensical, and at worst, unhelpful and de-motivational. All you need for success is a genuine interest in a topic and the persistence to develop skills which can create value for other people. In this new paradigm of achievement, I encourage you to focus all your energy on how you can provide value for other people and completely forget about how you compare to others in your field. Make sure that whatever you're working on aligns with your values and interests and isn't primarily intended to impress others. Anything you do that brings you a sense of joy will resonate positively with everyone around you.

It's important to revisit the distinction between being and doing. Some people label themselves and others as "somebodies" and "nobodies". This sort of labeling is unhelpful because it's usually used in a judgmental context. What's worse, is that it promotes a dubious paradigm of achievement. Someone who strives to "become a somebody" in life is doing so from a feeling of low self-worth and measures themselves based on the opinions of others. That paradigm comes from the idea that some people have higher innate worth than others. In contrast, I believe that all human beings have equal value and that all human life is sacred. Your focus should be on doing something significant which benefits others and captivates your interest and enthusiasm. The person you are today is already perfect. If you keep your focus on doing great things for others, you'll accrue lasting personal benefits.

If what you love doing doesn't provide any value to anyone else but you, it's a hobby, not a career. The companies that produce the goods and services we use every day accomplish incredible achievements because they deliver value to people every day. These companies endure because they provide essential products and services. Their efforts maintain the backbone for modern life. I encourage you to reevaluate your goals and aspirations in terms of how you can become an essential product or service provider in any field. You can serve niche fields or mainstream fields. Rather than striving to make a million dollars as a graphic artist, consider the goal of getting your artwork featured in a publication with a million readers. Rather than trying to hit $1 million in annual sales, consider the goal of selling to 5,000 customers in one year. Rather than using people as a means to your ends, make people the ends instead, and over time, your personal ends will come to fruition. Keep this question in mind as you evaluate your goals, "Whom am I serving and benefiting by accomplishing this goal?" The motivation you feel to accomplish a goal is much stronger when you're working for the benefit of others. The more people you can benefit, the better!

Your Higher Goal

No matter what activity you perform, as long as you're challenged enough to stretch beyond your currently abilities, you'll end up achieving a higher goal. The process you will have undergone while working on your goal: the ups and downs, the physical and emotional drama, the crises of confidence, and the late nights and early mornings leading up to your success, will have transformed you as an individual. Becoming the kind of person who can achieve a desired goal defines what it means to be "self-made".

You become a role model for those around you by who you become more so than by the result you achieve. For example, if one of your goals is to dunk a basketball, it won't be satisfying to you if the basketball hoop is lowered to eight feet. You'll be able to dunk it, but all the glory and value of the goal is gone. You'll need to strengthen your body and improve your athleticism enough to dunk in a standard ten-foot rim. Once you've improved your fitness to this point, you'll be able to dunk whenever you feel like it.

If someone were to give you a million dollars, it would come in handy for paying debts and buying things. But it wouldn't suddenly make you any more capable of earning a million dollars. To earn that much money, you need to develop and execute a good idea which delivers value to others. Once you've done this, you'll have made yourself into the kind of person who can earn money whenever necessary. It's the difference between giving a man a fish versus teaching him to fish. Achieving a worthy goal that you've identified elevates you as a person. You become more capable of achieving other challenging goals because of your experience and wisdom. For example, if you overcome the difficulties involved in starting a profitable business, not only does that make it easier for you to start another one, it also better prepares you mentally and emotionally for other challenges which require determination and persistence.

My dad once told me the old Armenian tale of "the golden bracelets". A merchant was traveling through the desert with all his goods packed on several camels when he was attacked by thieves. The thieves took everything he had and left him only his loincloth. As they were leaving, the merchant said to them, "You took everything except my golden bracelets!" They replied, "What bracelets? You have nothing left and you are all but naked." The merchant explained, "You can take all my possessions, but you can never take my golden bracelets. I have knowledge and skills which cannot be taken away. I will soon replace all those goods and return to my station in life. You, however, will sell those goods for less than they're worth and then squander the money. After you've done so, you'll still be thieves." The golden bracelets are a figurative device used to represent the merchant's skills and confidence, which are more valuable than physical wealth.

Success in your choice of endeavor isn't about getting something; it's about becoming the kind of person who can produce that something. A great chef can make a very good meal out of mediocre ingredients under difficult circumstances. Someone without cooking experience can't produce a good meal even with the best ingredients. Once you've built expertise in your area of interest and delivered meaningful value to other people, you'll find the intrinsic rewards far outweigh whatever you received in compensation and unlike the money, can never be taken away from you.

Being a certain type of person comes from practicing behaviors over and over until they become habits. Don't worry about trying to be a certain way. You can't control what you are. You can only control what you do. You can change what you're doing right now and start doing something new and different immediately. Once you've practiced a set of behaviors enough times that they become habitual, you will effectively be different from the person you were before by virtue of your new habits, skills, and knowledge. What new productive habits can you start cultivating today?

Failure Is a Weasel Word

Some people like to say, "There's no such thing as failure." They say this to encourage you to keep striving and to never give up. I appreciate their helpful motives but would like to offer a different point of view. There absolutely is such a thing as failure. The concept is ingrained in our society, but I choose to interpret it more skeptically than most. Failure is an emotionally charged mental construct designed to add formal importance and significance to people's not getting the result they wanted or not achieving something they set out to do. The concept of failure is a device people often unknowingly use to influence the way you think about something. The phrase "Failure is not an option." is equivalent to saying "Not getting exactly what I want is not an option." People characterize failure negatively so that when they don't get the result they were expecting, they can say that something "bad" happened and that this bad thing is now a problem for them and maybe even for you! I've attended company meetings where the executives announced, "Our company failed to meet its quarterly earnings targets." I'm always left thinking, "So what?", "Were they realistic?" and "And that's a problem for me because…?"

Whatever happens in the world as a result of your actions (as long as you're not harming anyone) is neutral. It's how you choose to think and feel about it that gives it meaning. Now, for someone intending to achieve a particular result, it's perfectly reasonable for that person to feel temporarily frustrated when that result isn't achieved. The problem lies in how the person labels that result. For example, in my mid-20s, I studied for the CPA exam and did not pass it the first time. I did indeed feel temporarily frustrated but I didn't label it as a "failure". I ended up passing it the second time after studying daily for three months using a better study strategy than before. If I'm playing a basketball game with friends and I shoot the ball and miss, I don't drop to my knees and cry out in misery about my "failure" even though I did intend to make the shot. I just realize that I didn't make it that time and I'll try again next time. It's often said Thomas Edison discovered ten thousand ways how not to design an incandescent light bulb. He didn't declare "failure" each time. Those were just learning steps along the path towards getting the first one to work.

I believe that whenever anyone talks to you about some "failure", they're trying to control you. They're simultaneously presenting a situation and the supposedly correct judgment of that situation. In the same breath, they're saying "This is what happened and it was bad." It's the same as if the defendant in a court case were referred to by the plaintiff as "that guilty person over there". They're trying, either consciously or subconsciously, to make your judgment for you by characterizing something as a failure before you've had the chance to evaluate the situation for yourself. Typically, they're disappointed with some outcome and they want you to also interpret that outcome as disappointing. They want you to be good company for their misery and even to share in their shame. For example, people who tell you they failed in school or in business may explain it as if the failure were due to some external force or set of circumstances beyond their control which forced them to give up. Natural disasters, market crashes and the like are the risks inherent in the world we live in. There's nothing wrong with giving up on something and trying something else. Evaluating what works and what doesn't is vital to your continued success. However, when someone characterizes something as a "failure", rather than as a learning experience, it is, at best, disingenuous and, at worst, manipulative. When people point the finger of failure at themselves it's just as unhelpful as when they point it at others.

You're an independent person, free to think and feel whatever you wish about any situation. Don't let people use the concept of failure to control your opinions or your feelings. In the same vein, you might reconsider how you use the word failure. It's a weasel word unbecoming of an enlightened person. Learn as much as you can from all your experiences, however you interpret them. Learning compounded with regular practice will bring you the results you're looking for. It may take longer than you'd like but will happen sooner than you think!

Chapter 2 Exercises

Exercise 1. Interview Role Models

Find two people in your community who have achieved something you consider impressive or admirable. You probably don't have to look very far. Interview them with the intention of learning about the following: the specific steps they took in their achievement, the setbacks they faced, the doubts they may have had, their mindset before and after, and the specific event or point at which they realized they had achieved their goal. After your interviews, reflect on what you learned and consider what you've already achieved and the specific process by which you did so. Are you facing career decisions at the current time? Consider how you can replicate your previous successes in your current situation.

Exercise 2. Reexamine Your Goals

Write your current achievement goals down on a piece of paper. Review each goal and ask the question, "Whom am I serving and benefiting through the accomplishment of this goal?" If the answer is no one but yourself or very few people, consider changing the goal to benefit more people. If the nature of your goal doesn't include many other people, find a few people with whom you can share your goal and ask them to hold you accountable. If your goal concerns a sum of money, consider changing it so that serving other people is the focus and the money is a byproduct of the people's satisfaction.

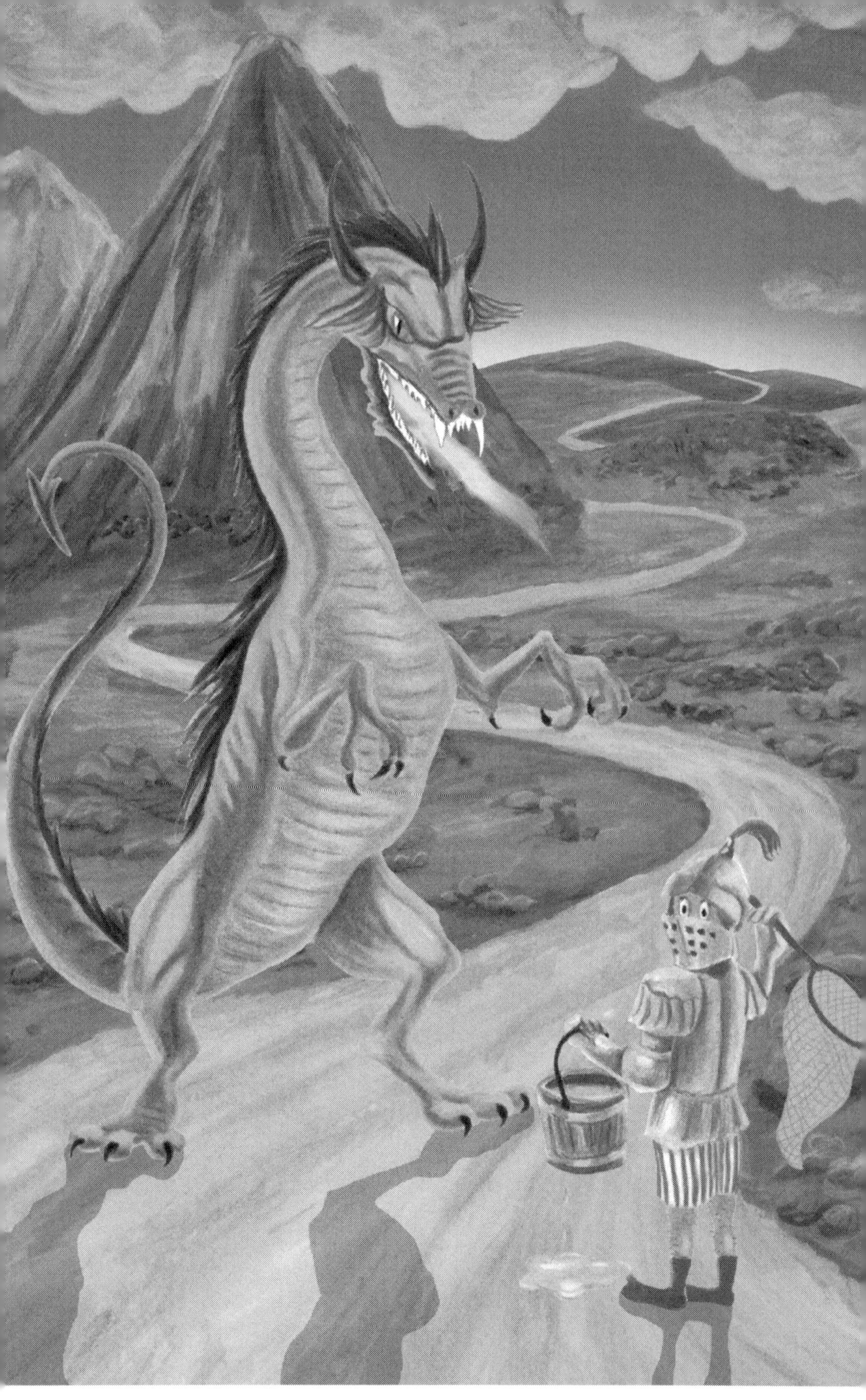

Chapter 3

Education

The current financial cost of a typical four-year college degree has risen to levels which call into question its value. The loans many college students sign up for hobble their financial progress for decades. What is it about college that costs so much money? One of the ways colleges become more prestigious is by building larger and larger buildings which are very expensive to maintain but look beautiful in glossy brochures and websites. The way these institutions function financially and operationally hasn't seemed to change at all since I was in college in the 1990s despite their access to transformative new technology. These institutions continue to have a vested interest in their architecture, grounds, and other pricey physical artifacts which contribute little to learning.

Only a small proportion of areas of study and occupation require grandiose, costly architectural structures, laboratories, and specialized tools which would justify such a high cost. Most of the things you'll end up learning and working on in your career don't require elaborate, expensive equipment and can be learned at home (often for free). You don't need to attend classes at some campus that looks like a medieval castle or some fancy property on the Las Vegas Strip, in order to study in your field of interest.

We are taught that higher education is the path that makes success possible. Indeed, college graduates, as a whole, earn significantly more money over the course of their careers than people who did not attend college. What we are not taught, however, is the process of determining what to study in college, and why. This chapter won't tell you what to study, but it will help you think about how to make your choices. The majority of graduates work in fields different from what they studied in college. This doesn't necessarily mean the time and money they spent on college was completely wasted, but it could have been much better optimized had they spent more time discovering themselves and choosing majors more strategically.

The types of higher education available today include:

Formal university
Community college
Online college degrees
Distance education
Online Continuing Education
Trade schools
Professional certifications
On the job training/Internships
University extension classes
Massive Open Online Courses

The options are numerous, complex and confusing. The cost of each varies greatly and the benefits of each with respect to the others aren't fully clear. You'd likely need to complete some higher education course just to understand the pros and cons of all the options! The best course of action is to define more specifically one's areas of interest through some of the less expensive options before committing to the more expensive ones. I can't tell you what subject to study or how you should study it. What this chapter does do, however, is promote the following idea about education: *Make sure your education provides you with lots of valuable skills and options.*

Redshirting

The term "redshirting" refers to the practice in American collegiate football of extending a student-athlete's education to include a fifth year and delaying eligibility for participation in the sport until the second year. This allows the player to practice with the team for the first year to improve his strength, skills and experience. It also allows him to get used to college life before taking on the challenge of managing both academics and football. The player's eligibility then begins the second year and lasts for four years, the final one being when the player is considered a "fifth-year senior."

If you're still in school, the concept of redshirting can be applied to the approach you take to your career no matter what academic stage you're in. It's unrealistic to think that most young people know with enough certainty the areas of interest that they would like to pursue to justify the large financial expenditure necessary for college. How many people do you know that actually work in the field they majored in during college? I recommend, for all but the most certain young people, to take some time after high school to get as much exposure as possible to a variety of work and life experiences. Most diligent high school students lead very busy lives with their coursework, sports, school events, friends, and extracurricular activities. Beyond studying the academic aspects of a particular subject, many high school students likely have not put in enough quality time in diverse areas of interest to confidently know what to study and commit tens of thousands of dollars to it in college. Students in many countries take a "gap year" to get to know themselves and their interests better before continuing with college. I recommend a gap year plus a year or two in community college to gain maximum exposure to many areas of study which may interest you. Exploring personal interests and developing useful skills are more important than earning high grades, starting work early, or finishing college on time. A few extra years of self-exploration before entering college will pay off big in terms of your academic choices and the value of the money spent on your formal education.

Just because you're you doesn't mean you understand yourself profoundly. There have been many instances in which I thought I knew enough about something to rule it out as an interest, only for my wife to prove me wrong and chuckle about it later. Discuss your aspirations with friends and family, if they're receptive, to get third-party perspectives on your ideas. They may try to direct you into areas which don't interest you or discourage you from those that do. Respect their advice even if you realize you don't intend to follow it. It may prove difficult to identify a specific career interest early in life. Or, you may identify one, spend a bunch of time and money on it, and later realize it's not for you. If this happens to you, don't fret. All knowledge is related and it's likely it will come in handy someday, but try to avoid this if possible. Start with a general area that you've been interested in like business or science or health care and gain exposure to as many different aspects as possible to see what interests you. There are dozens of different areas to explore in each of these broad subjects.

After college, I worked in a long series of temporary jobs. The most valuable thing I learned from them was that many jobs I was qualified for, I didn't like! Most people view a job loss as a negative life event. The truth is, it's a great opportunity to fine-tune your career by exposing yourself to as many new areas as possible through temporary work. You don't have to identify anything specific right away, the right decision should feel right to you.

College is a Time, Not a Place

Most people think of college as a physical location where people go to study, usually for only four years. College brochures and websites reinforce this idea of college as a place with beautiful photographs of the campus grounds and fancy buildings. From the colleges' point of view, these properties and facilities are quite expensive to maintain and they devote a percentage of the tuition you pay to maintain these very physical artifacts which show off the college. How necessary are these physical artifacts to your learning?

I prefer to think of college as a period of time, or a season in your life during which your primary activity is studying academic subjects of your choice. This time is special and you should spend most of it studying rather than working, if possible. You have the rest of your life to work! I think of it as a time rather than a place because it doesn't matter where you go to college; what matters is how much you learn that you can put to good use afterwards. In college, choosing a major shouldn't be a "major decision." You should have multiple areas of interest and no single one should take precedence over the others so early in your career. Your minors should be as important to you as your majors. In undergrad you're barely scratching the surface of any topic you study. You're still discovering each subject's various facets, which topics interest you, and how they might manifest into future work. This is the time of your life in which you should be exposing yourself to as many options as possible, not limiting yourself in any way by focusing too much on one major area of study.

If I could do college over again, I would choose a much less expensive school and study for much longer. Four years is not enough time to learn all the academic subjects which both interest me and could benefit me for the rest of my life, personally and professionally. Based on my personal and career interests, if I could go back in time to my college years, I would double-major in computer science and statistics and have a quadruple-minor in Spanish, French, music, and business. It wouldn't matter to me if it took six years or more to complete, rather than the standard four years. If I could get financial aid and scholarships, it's likely I would graduate with a similar amount of debt or less than if I'd gone to a more expensive school for only four years. The difference, however, is that I would have gotten a massively better education. The fact that I would be 24 or 25 years old or older when I graduated, rather than 22, makes no difference at all. Considering all the skills I would have acquired, the time would have been extremely well spent. A broader undergraduate background with two or more majors and two or more minors would prepare you for a much wider variety of options for graduate school and subsequent careers.

Which college you attend is far less important than you think. What's more important is finding subjects you enjoy which also give you as many skills and options as possible. Devote much of your extra time in college to discovering academic interests you may enjoy which you haven't yet considered. Assume that your assumptions about any subject you've ever heard of are incorrect. They probably are! And those assumptions could be holding you back from something you have no idea would be of immense interest to you. Try to audit as many classes as possible, not for credit. Audit some classes which are more advanced than your current level just to see what they're about and if they appeal to you. Spend as much time as you can learning valuable skills that you'll be able to use for the rest of your life. Learn to play a musical instrument or sing or paint or program a computer or learn a foreign language. Visit your professors often and engage them in conversation; they'll be delighted by your genuine interest. Years later you'll remember and appreciate all the time you spent with them. Spend as much time in college as you can to make sure you cover all your academic interests. This includes ones you already know you have and ones you've yet to discover. Once you enter the workforce and take on more life responsibilities, it will be much harder to go back to school and give it the attention it deserves.

Creating Options for Yourself

The work you do is a delicate balance between your skills and interests and what society values as worthy of compensation. As a young person, you may not have a profound certainty about the best way for you to provide value and earn a living. In my jobs, I've worked with many high-level corporate executives. For the most part, they have one and only one job - to make decisions. They're faced with important, often expensive decisions, not unlike your decision about what work to do. I've noticed that they all behave in pretty much the same way. Executives, in all their dealings, strive to open as many options as possible, for as long as possible. This includes decisions about whom to hire and fire, which vendors to choose, which products to buy, who gets promoted, and how to spend money. Executives rarely do any "work" themselves, as their main job is to make decisions about the future of the company. To an executive, the cost of making an error can be very high - to the company and to his career. The primary way executives mitigate this risk is by having lots of options available at all times.

You'll eventually decide what types of work to pursue. Then you'll spend time improving your skills in order to increase the value you're able to offer. You'll want to have high-quality offerings that can be easily explained and understood. You'll want to advance to higher levels of value delivered, responsibility, and compensation. Rather than enduring a long string of low-paying entry-level jobs, ensure that the opportunities you choose will build skills you can leverage at work which are also personally edifying. If you have to choose between one job opportunity that pays more money and another which will help you build a valuable skill, choose the latter. Learning the skill will be more fulfilling in the short term and more valuable to you in your portfolio in the future. Treat your daily work with a playful attitude and consider yourself an artist or craftsman perfecting your trade.

You should find areas whose soft and hard skills require intense training to master. Any truly valuable skills are only acquired after thorough practice, which may take years. Envision yourself working on challenging problems day after day and experiencing your share of difficulty, frustration, glory, and learning. Early on, it is not necessary to zero in on anything extremely specific. In fact, unless you're positive about what you'd like to do for your life's work, specifying something too early can limit your options later. Instead, focus on skills you'd like to gain and improve upon, and those that give you more options later. The field I work in, business intelligence, didn't really exist when I was in high school. Keeping my options open made it available to me later in life by adding a set of extra skills that helped me reinvent my career after grad school. Get exposure to as many areas as possible and learn skills which will give you the most future options.

I enjoy speaking foreign languages. I'm proficient in Spanish, Italian, and French. Quite a few people have told me, "I took four years of Spanish in high school and I'm frustrated that I can't speak much of it." I always ask them, "How many hours have you actually spent speaking Spanish?" Learning a skill is kind of like getting an airline pilot's license. It requires a certain number of hours of actual flying. People have also told me, "I practiced speaking Spanish with my friend but it felt so difficult and painful, and I felt so unskilled." The pain and awkwardness they experienced was the learning process taking place. The more you exert yourself, even though you feel awkward, the better you'll get. If you keep it up over time, one day you'll wake up and say, "Yo hablo español!" A mentor once told me that the most skilled programmers are the ones who've made the most mistakes. This reflects my experiences with speaking foreign languages, programming computers, and roller skating. My skills at these were awkward, clumsy, and unrefined for long periods of time and I still often experience difficult moments. However, after much practice, I'm very happy and comfortable with these areas, and I'm still improving. Unless you're independently wealthy, you will have to work for a living. Proficiency in a difficult skill will give you options unavailable to others. Choose something that will challenge you and make you feel awkward and uncomfortable at first. The more difficult it is in the beginning, the more glorious you will feel when you succeed.

Synergistic Disciplines

The correlation between grades and career success is dubious, despite what your teachers and family may tell you. It's true that those who have reached the highest levels of their fields, especially those which require high levels of academic expertise like science, medicine, engineering, and computing, have their choice of the best opportunities available. But for the rest of us, there remains another more accessible avenue to attain similar levels of success - synergistic disciplines. If you can develop competency in a combination of complementary or synergistic areas, you will be uniquely positioned to take advantage of multidisciplinary opportunities. Having education and experience in different but related disciplines allows you to see the same problem from multiple perspectives and use combinations of different tools to attack a problem from all sides. Most people envision the pursuit of a career as a kind of "hero's journey" through a series of challenges towards a predefined success. A better analogy though would be a hero's scavenger hunt. Many successful people have meandered through a series of vastly different areas, trying to coordinate their diverse interests with some way to make a living.

In high school and college I got decent grades, but I was never a straight-A student. I wanted to do well, and excelled in my foreign language classes, but for whatever reason I never made high grades a priority. I've performed well in my work despite not having excellent grades because I enjoy what I do and because I work in a field which combines three synergistic disciplines - business, computer programming, and statistical analysis. Because of low grades in my accounting major, I received no interest from any of the then "Big 6" accounting firms with whom I interviewed. I studied marketing in graduate school and my first job afterwards involved programming databases for a container shipping firm. In all my jobs since then I continued programming databases and I later earned a graduate certificate in an area of statistics. Working in these synergistic areas has been enjoyable and lucrative. I rarely have trouble finding work because each subject area is in demand and the combination of them is even more so. Below are some examples of combinations of useful skills or disciplines that go well together, and an example of what someone with these skills can do.

- Medicine and Computer Science - Create new medical devices and technology.
- Computer Programming and Accounting - Automate time-consuming tasks and reduce errors.
- Dietitian and Chef – Design and prepare healthy, tasty meals for people in a variety of settings.
- Education and Business - Train workers and businesspeople to be more productive and cooperative.
- Law and Computing - Help legislators understand the effects of new technology; manage privacy, patents, and intellectual property.
- Biology and Semiconductor Technology - Develop mobile medical devices to diagnose and treat people in remote locations.
- Biology and Engineering - Apply bioengineering to develop new therapies, medicines, and imaging techniques.

It takes longer to gain expertise in multiple fields and you may have to spend more time and money in college. You may also have to delay when you start working. However, if you gain a valuable combination of complementary skills like the ones above, you create a very desirable professional profile and a barrier to entry to those who might compete for similar opportunities. Your skills in each area may not be comparable to those at the very highest levels of each field, but your combination of synergistic skills will be valuable and formidable. Can you think of some skills you could obtain that would complement the ones you already have?

Chapter 3 Exercises

Exercise 1. Career Conversations

You're probably connected to a diverse set of people: your friends, the people you work with, and those from different generations. Pick one or two people from each group and ask them how they came to work in their careers. Once you've heard what they have to say, explain your story to them and ask for feedback. You may be surprised to find out they have a friend or relative who has a similar interest to yours and they may be able to put you in contact with that person. They may have perspectives on avenues you hadn't considered. The mere act of discussing this with many people can stimulate your mind and make you more receptive to new ideas.

Exercise 2. Job Shadowing

Research local companies or organizations corresponding to areas of interest you have. Call them up and explain that you're a student or member of the community and that you're interested in their area of operation. Request that they allow you to visit them on site and participate in their activity, free of charge, as a learning experience. If they aren't willing to let you actively participate, request that they allow you to interview a few employees informally. Some companies may deny your request but if you keep calling around, you'll eventually find someone who'll be willing to let you visit them. You may have to take time off from school or work to do this but it may prove well worth your time.

Exercise 3. Get Qualified

On the left side of a piece of paper, write down a list of all the career-related skills in which you currently have competency. Examples might be technical writing, contract negotiation, account management, and training. On the right side, write the names of jobs for which you're currently qualified. Some examples might be legal assistant, Naval Fire Control Technician, database developer, and graphic designer. Connect each skill on the left with the corresponding job on the right by drawing a line between them. Which of your skills connects to the most jobs and which ones connect to the least jobs? Do you already have some skills now that would apply to jobs which may interest you but for which you're not yet fully qualified? Consider skills you could add to the left side which would make more jobs appear on the right side. Consider jobs you'd like to add on the right side which would require new skills on the left side. Can any of the jobs on the right side be combined to take advantage of more of your skills? How might you market yourself as someone with skills in multiple disciplines who can approach problems in novel ways?

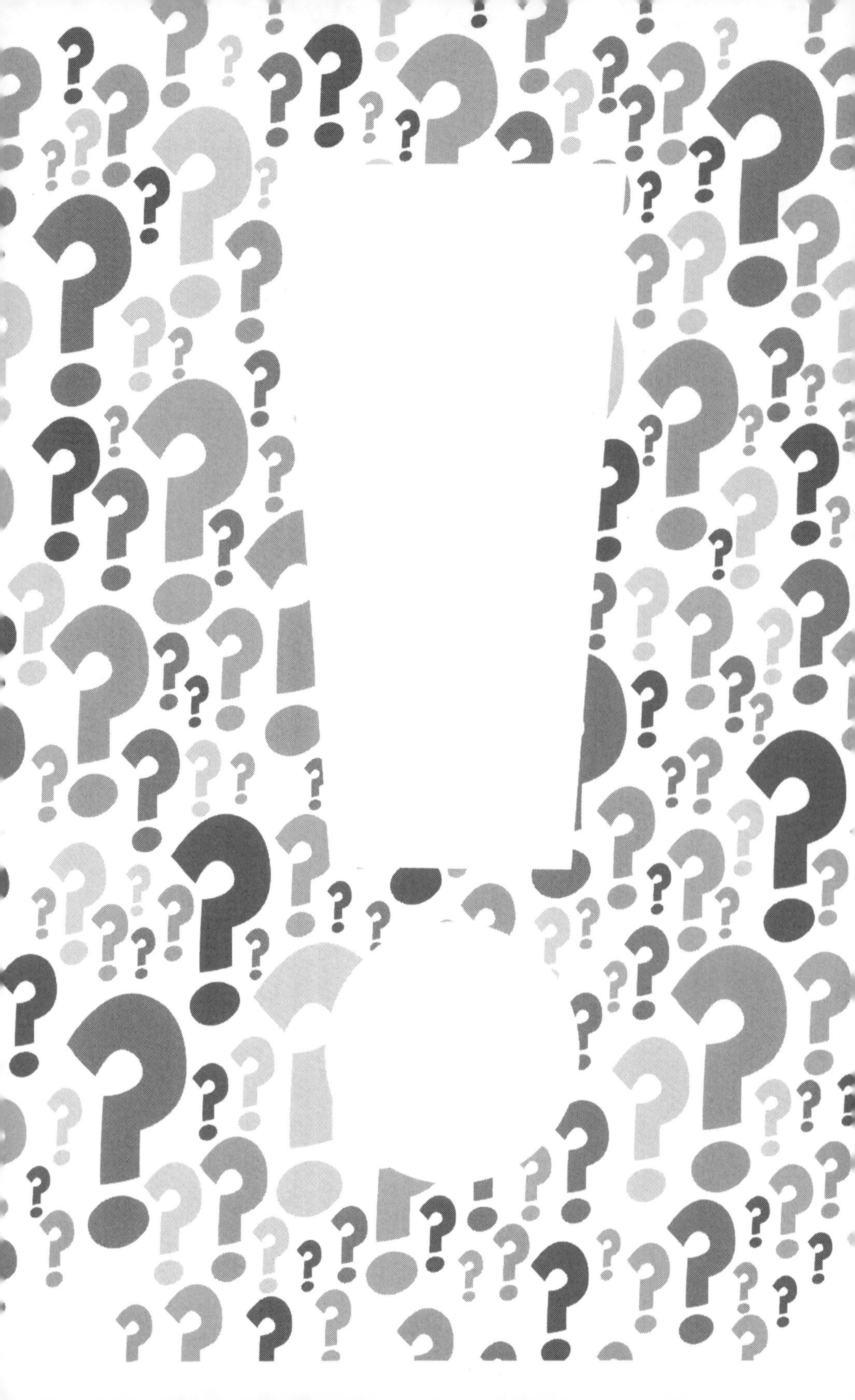

Chapter 4
Self Confidence

Because almost any activity you engage in will involve other people, how they perceive your personality is essential to consider when creating opportunities for yourself. When assessing candidates for jobs, investment, or other opportunities, after determining whether they possess the necessary technical skills and experience, decision makers choose the person they like most. That's what human resource professionals are referring to when they use the word "fit." It's as much a popularity contest as it is a meritocracy. Not only are interviewers concerned with whether a candidate can do a job, they're concerned with whether they would enjoy working with that person, whether that person will be taken seriously by the rest of the company, and how well they will reflect on the hiring manager.

So what causes decision-makers to choose one person over another? They are looking for two specific kinds of confidence: confidence in your skills and ability and confidence in social situations. Your job as an interview candidate is to help the interviewers make the case to the business that you're the best candidate for the job. When faced with multiple candidates, interviewers are looking for ways to make their decisions easier. If you dress unprofessionally or display any flaky behavior, you'll be weeded out right away. Human resources staff and hiring managers are putting their professional reputations on the line when they present you to their businesses. The same is true with potential clients when you own your own business. They need to feel at ease with you and know you'll support their needs. Make sure your offerings are fully developed and well-presented. Your appearance and behavior must inspire confidence and enthusiasm.

Once you get the interview, you're no longer competing against the other candidates as much as you're helping to prove to the interviewers that they've chosen the right person. At the end of the meeting, it should be totally obvious to everyone in the room that you're a great choice because you possess the complete package of skills and personality they need. Your job is to transfer your high level of confidence in yourself to the interviewers so they have that same confident feeling when they're selling their hiring decision to the rest of management.

In several interviews, I've been asked why I thought I was the best candidate. This is a silly question. I always answer that I have no idea whether I'm the best candidate because I know nothing about the other candidates. Then I explain I'm a great candidate based on what's stated on the job description and on what I know they're looking for. My honesty is usually appreciated and interpreted as confidence. I deliver my spiel in my unique way, and they either like me or they don't. At the end of the interview, I know I've done it my way. If the company didn't choose me, it just means our personalities didn't mesh and it wouldn't have been a good fit for either of us. This chapter challenges you to evaluate your current level of confidence and presents ideas for how you can be perceived as confident by others. I encourage you to *identify and perfect your personal style to gain confidence in yourself and your potential.*

Your Unique Personal Mojo

Everyone has a unique personal style or mojo, whether or not it's intentional. What not everyone has is a good understanding of what makes their style unique. Would you be able to objectively describe your personal style? Would your description match what those around you would say? If you're not fully aware by now of which personality type you fit into, consider taking a personality test like the Myers-Briggs test or the Birkman Method. The ability to comfortably engage new people in social or career situations is extremely valuable. Opportunities can appear in places where you least expect them, and it pays to be ready to introduce yourself to someone new and make a good impression right away. Perfecting your unique personal style makes you more comfortable when interacting with new people because you're well-rehearsed in introducing yourself and breaking the ice.

For example, if you're shy you may best interact with new people after a formal introduction from someone you already know. If you're a little more daring, you may learn that all you need to do is find some plausible reason to talk to someone you don't know so your interaction doesn't feel too contrived. If you're totally fearless in social situations, you may be able to walk up to someone you've never met and just say hello and introduce yourself. Perfecting your unique methods for meeting new people will help you get the most exposure. If you're currently not a very social person, you might benefit from some form of training in how to break the ice with people and engage them in social conversation. There are many great courses and books which teach you to reduce your fear of social situations and learn to effectively engage with new people. The benefits of mastering this skill include creating new relationships and opportunities, making progress on your goals by involving other people, inspiring people to offer you better deals and access to resources, lowering peoples' inhibitions, and making lasting positive impressions.

A big part of my personal style is the ability to make conventionally mundane situations humorous or silly. When I go to a restaurant which has a smoking section, and the host asks me if I'd like "smoking or nonsmoking", I always respond with, "I'll take second-hand smoking please!" Sometimes when I go to the grocery store, I'll ask the cashier if I can "put the groceries on layaway." At the barber shop, I'll sometimes ask the barber for "hair extensions" or a hairstyle which "will cause women in public to stop what they're doing and give me their phone numbers." At coffee shops, just to start a funny conversation, I'll ask the barista to tell me the largest number of artificial sweetener packets a customer has ever asked him to put in a drink. The highest number I've heard so far is 17! I once helped a guy I met at a coffee shop apply for a job which required a letter of interest. Rather than help him write the typical letter explaining why he wanted the job, I encouraged him to write a fictitious letter from the company to him explaining why they were interested in him and why they thought he was such a great candidate. I'm sure it was the most unique letter of interest that company received.

Expressing your unique personality in a creative way makes an impact and separates you from the crowd. I realize these examples are quite cheesy, but that's my personality and it makes me feel confident, funny, and happy. To engage people in in your own unique way both requires and builds confidence. The more you do it the easier it gets. Your improved ability to communicate with others helps you get special treatment and benefits based on the rapport you build. I've heard many interesting stories and made new friends by breaking the ice and acting in fun, unconventional ways. Believe me, this is totally "a thing" and it works!

Confidence Success Multiplier

A theme I've noticed regarding success is that the most opportunities and resources flow to those who seem to need them the least. This theme is so prevalent that it even exists in the Bible. The book of St. Matthew contains the quote, "For whoever has, to him more shall be given, and he will have an abundance; but whoever does not have, even what he has shall be taken away from him." Another way of putting this is the quote, "Nothing succeeds like success." The higher an executive is in a company, the more tangible and intangible benefits that person receives in the form of annual bonuses not shared by lower level employees, free meals, free airfare and hotel rooms, frequent flier miles, gifts, discounted or free company products and services, comped entertainment from the company or its vendors, and access to better networking opportunities which lead to more lucrative future employment. I read a statistic recently that the world's top eighty-five wealthiest people are worth more financially than the bottom fifty percent of all people on earth! People in these positions gain confidence from their successes and then more success from their confidence. I call this the "confidence success multiplier effect." It acts as a positive feedback loop. The more confidence someone has, the more opportunities he receives to increase his financial and emotional security. The more security he has, the more risks he can take which yield greater financial rewards, which in turn build more confidence. This effect snowballs over time, delivering to the confident person much of what he desires in life.

Prospective employers and people in positions to offer you opportunities can sense even the slightest vibes of neediness and desperation in the way you present yourself. They want to hire and promote people they find impressive, confident, and in demand. They want to feel like they swiped you off the market, got a great deal, and cheated their competitors out of the opportunity to have your services. If an employer hires you because you were the least undesirable option or because they're taking a chance on an unproven person who's grateful to have the job, you'll have low levels of respect and leverage in negotiations. A prospective boss once asked me why I was interested in working for his company. I told him I wasn't particularly interested yet, but since his recruiter had called me and piqued my curiosity, I'd decided to attend the interview. I told him and the human resources person what my real interests were, and that if such and such other duties would be required, that I probably wasn't the right candidate. I got the feeling that the more I resisted, the more the company wanted to hire me. I accepted the job after negotiating a sizable pay increase as well as a higher job title than what the company had originally advertised.

Financial security creates a level of safety, comfort, and confidence that can be challenging to achieve without it. However, if you're not financially secure, you can still create this emotional state within yourself and project it to others. I've benefitted from this confidence success multiplier effect by leveraging positions of emotional security, even when my financial situation may not have inspired confidence. When you don't need a job and are considering it solely based on how it aligns with your interests, you project an attractive confidence to employers which allows you to negotiate from a position of strength. I was fortunate enough live with my parents until I was twenty-six years old. Because I didn't have to pay rent and expenses, I was able to experience the effects of this confidence and I was in the position of being able to turn down opportunities I didn't like - even if I had to hide this from my parents who would have been disappointed if they had found out!

My dad once drove me to an interview for an accounting job during the winter in Virginia when there was over a foot of snow on the ground and my hand-me-down station wagon probably wouldn't have made it. He waited for me in his work truck in the parking lot outside while I attended the interview. The interviewers told me the job would involve both accounts payable and accounts receivable. It all seemed very tedious and not to my liking. The trouble was, I got the feeling they really liked me and I was afraid they would call me at home and offer me the job. I knew my parents would be upset if I turned down the offer. This was before the era of ubiquitous cell phones and I wouldn't have been able to have a private conversation on our house phone. So, when the interview was over, I called the number on the interviewer's business card from the pay phone in the lobby. I explained who I was, thanked her for the interview, and told her that I didn't want the job. I felt nervous turning down the job minutes after the interview, but relieved that I'd "dodged a bullet."

I once got a temp job at a company which had hired two other temps for a database project. The company representative spent about ten minutes explaining the database issue. He'd figured that if he divided the problem into three parts, one for each temp, that we could do the job three times faster. Upon hearing the specifics of the database project, I realized it wasn't a three-person job and that I could solve this problem in a few hours by myself. I tried to explain this in multiple ways to the company representative, but he wasn't the slightest bit convinced. Right then and there I decided to walk off the job rather than stay in a situation with an unreasonable manager. On my way home, I stopped at my favorite bookstore and met a beautiful young woman and we began dating. The confidence that allowed me to leave that job extended to my successful meeting in the bookstore.

Turning down opportunities which aren't right for you or persuading someone to change an opportunity so that it meets your specifications will create a critical shift in the mindset with which you approach any job search. It also turns the tables on your relationships with prospective employers and puts you in a better bargaining position. The feelings of confidence and security clear the pathway for better opportunities. By saying no, you're telling the world that you're free to pick and choose the best opportunities on your terms. You're also affirming that many opportunities exist for you and that you live in a world of abundance rather than of lack. You're proclaiming that the only "scarce resource" in your world is you. You're not the type of person who's forced to accept the first thing that comes along. Not only are great opportunities available for you to choose, you have the power to create opportunities for yourself whenever you like. The next time you show up to begin a new project, give it enough of a chance for you to get past any initial unfamiliarity or apprehension you may have. Then ask yourself how this experience feels to you and whether the work and people involved are fundamentally reasonable and worth your time. If you feel an uncomfortable or unfriendly vibe, trust your judgment and leave gracefully.

People who project confidence based on their expertise, qualifications, and professional behavior command high compensation. People in positions of power perceive that confident people deserve more and pay them more. At one company where I worked, I had the opportunity to work with temporary employees as well as highly paid consultants on the same project. The management had no problem paying the consultants more than fifteen times the hourly rate of the temporary employees and acted generously towards the consultants and stingily toward the temps. When I asked why the managers paid so much to the consultants and so little to the temps, they had numerous ways of rationalizing the obvious inequity. None of the reasons they cited, however, justified the extent of the difference in pay. Ultimately, I concluded that it was the clever way the consultants intentionally sold the value of their services to the company. The temps were operating from a mindset of weakness and lack; they accepted what they were offered by the company even when they were in good bargaining positions. From their point of view, they couldn't afford to haggle with the big company for fear of losing their already meager wages. You can't succeed with that mindset. You mustn't let yourself get into a situation where you have to take what you're offered and there's no room for negotiation. By the sheer force of your personality, character, and expertise, you must project convincingly that you will only accept high pay and that you will deliver even higher value in return. The profit margin on some modern smartphones is huge, yet we pay it happily because of the value the phones provide us. If you successfully demonstrate your expertise, you will be able to exchange the high value of your services for high levels of pay.

To start making this confidence multiplier effect work in your favor, determine how you can alter your lifestyle to reduce stress and fear. It's hard to feel confident if you're afraid to lose your job because you're living paycheck to paycheck. Honestly examine your motives for being in your current job situation. Did you take your current job because you needed the money or did you honestly choose it based on your preferences? Work with a financial advisor to reduce your debt and expenses as much as possible and maximize your savings and investments. Decrease your "burn rate" (total monthly expenses) as much as possible. If you're paying a high rent or mortgage in order to live on your own, consider getting a roommate who can share the expenses. If you have alternate living opportunities, like with your parents or other generous family members, consider that any loss of autonomy you would experience while living with them would be made up for by the freedom it will give you to turn down sub-optimal choices. If you do choose to live with family or roommates, use this time as wisely as possible to secure the best situation for yourself. Put the extra money you were paying in rent into a savings account for a rainy day. The smaller your financial burden, the choosier you can afford to be with the opportunities you attract.

There is a distinct difference between projecting confidence and cockiness. Cockiness is off-putting and unattractive. Confidence is always welcome. I was once accused by a boss of acting overly cocky during an interview. He was right; I had pushed the envelope too far. It was painful for me to hear but was a valuable lesson. I still cringe when I think about it. My wife helped me understand this issue better. She told me to honestly examine my feelings and intentions. Confidence feels like you're explaining your true feelings in a matter-of-fact way with no intention beyond informing your audience of what you really want. Cockiness feels like showboating, like you're trying to impress your audience. Don't make the mistake I did by acting cocky; it's unbecoming of an enlightened person and disrespects your audience. The way to ensure you project confidence but not cockiness is to focus your effort on communicating authentically. I can't over-emphasize the beneficial effects of cultivating and projecting feelings of relaxed confidence. It will multiply your success!

Attitude, Not Aptitude

While watching my kids or their friends try something new for the first time, I've heard them say, "I'm not good at that." They seem to think if they try something a few times and don't have immediate positive results, it means they'll never be competent in that skill because of some inherent ability they lack. I read a book that said you shouldn't tell your children they're "smart" because doing so implies that intelligence is some innate trait rather than an ability that can be gained through study and effort. I agree; and when I talk to my kids about learning new things and what it means to be skillful in something, I equate it with the level of effort they're willing to expend. I encourage more practice and less judging.

A few years ago I decided to take up roller skating. I'd skated about half a dozen times when I was much younger and had felt intimidated by all the other people who could skate so fast around the rink and skate backwards and do tricks. I've found that I can be a slow beginner in some areas but if I give myself enough time, I can eventually advance to higher levels than those who sprinted ahead of me beforehand. At first, I started by skating for a few weeks in the street in front of my house. I would skate while pushing my big rolling trash can for balance. I looked ridiculous! Eventually, I had enough courage to go to my local rink. I went regularly for weeks and took Saturday morning classes. My movements were awkward and I spent as much time stumbling as I did skating. One afternoon after several weeks of practice, it occurred to me, "I'm really skating now!" Even now I can feel myself getting better every time I skate and I continue to practice new skills each time. In the years since I began, I've learned to skate backwards and sideways, and do several tricks. I'm now a competent skater and it feels great!

Eager to evaluate the progress of their pursuits, many people make premature judgments about their potential competency. To their detriment, they underestimate their abilities in a longer-term context, which holds them back from achieving their goals. How much you enjoy something will determine both the amount and quality of time you spend on it, which translates into competency over time. Pay no attention to others or even your own evaluation of your aptitude as a means of ruling something out. Early judgments of aptitude are largely unhelpful and irrelevant. If you enjoy something, your aptitude will grow over time. Aptitude should play a role in pointing you towards potential options but should not be used for ruling them out. Pay extra attention to things which come easily and quickly to you. They may represent good opportunities. But never rule out any areas you enjoy just because your skills aren't advanced today.

Perseverance in your topic of choice will both reveal and fill your gaps in ability. The more you learn, the more you realize that you originally knew less than you thought. This realization is your proper introduction to that topic. Once you fill in the gaps, you will build real expertise and will be able to capitalize on that new knowledge and skill. You must begin with a specific understanding of what you don't know (what gaps you're trying to fill) and then build upon the areas of your subject most useful to you. The confidence you build is based both on what you know now and on what you can learn when you need to. Your faith in yourself should be based on your ability to learn, not necessarily your current knowledge base. I'd much rather hire someone who doesn't know a skill but has high levels of confidence and willingness to learn, over someone who has the skill but lacks enthusiasm. True confidence comes from your willingness to learn and honest evaluations of yourself. The less natural talent you have for something, the more enthusiasm you will need because you will have to expend more effort in its mastery. In most cases where peoples' results have fallen short of their expectations, it was their enthusiasm that gave out before their ability.

When it comes to learning, it's your enthusiasm and direction which matter rather than the grades you get in school. A grade on a test is a single measurement at a specific time regarding whether you can answer a specific set of questions without help from reference materials like books or the internet. A grade is not a final judgment on your competency in that subject. It's not the final word on whether you'll ever understand or master a topic. A grade reflects whether at a particular time you could answer a specific set of questions. That's it. So many people internalize grades to mean things like, "I'm no good at math." or, "I got an A on my chemistry exam so I must be good at chemistry." In undergrad I got a D in my statistics class so I had to repeat it in grad school and received an A. Was I bad at stats back in undergrad and somehow got better in grad school? Not really, I studied more in grad school and performed better on the tests. My current skill in statistics comes mainly from the real-world projects I've worked on, not from the grades in my classes.

I'm convinced I was the worst student in an introductory Perl programming class I took at UC Berkeley Extension. I just didn't understand the concepts right away. After that class was over, I bought a book, read it cover to cover and did all the exercises. This gave me a much better understanding. Before I was finished reading it I had a great opportunity to apply it in my job. I spent three weeks writing a program to automate a tedious task. The program made one person's job much less stressful for an entire week each month. I became a programmer because I enjoyed it and I had real-world problems to solve. After finishing the program, I felt incredible. I didn't receive a grade for that project but instead received personal satisfaction and confidence from solving a problem that improved someone's life.

Personal Pacing

While the term personal mojo used earlier in this chapter refers to the energy you project into the world as you carry out your daily agenda, personal pacing refers to how you respond to the moment to moment changes presented to you by your environment. It pertains to how you react to what happens while you're carrying out your agenda, especially when it's unexpected. How do you react when you're interrupted by something or someone? How do you react when something you're working on doesn't turn out as you'd expected? You're living in the real world, and from moment to moment it's constantly teaching you lessons about reality, and about what works and what doesn't. To the degree that you respond with frustration, irritation, and complaints, you allow stress to overtake your mindset and corrupt your results.

Your typical reactions to stress reflect poorly on you and kill your mojo in the eyes of others. Frustration also limits the energy and creativity available for you to use to resolve the interruption. If you struggle with reacting to stress, it likely means that you have trouble mustering the energy or the will to accept the present moment as it is. Your resistance creates more unnecessary stress and obstacles than if you were to accept the situation and allow yourself to think creatively about it. Many great books on philosophy cover the topic of acceptance and can help you learn to diffuse stressful situations before they escalate. When something happens to me that I didn't expect and seems to be getting in the way of my personal agenda, I like to ask myself the question, "How can I make this situation work in my favor?" I must be honest though, sometimes frustrating things happen to me, and I'll recall this question with even more frustration. Sometimes I'd prefer to feel frustrated rather than ask myself a smart-aleck question! I'll ask myself the question anyway and usually come up with a good answer. At the very least, even if something does get in the way of your agenda and you're not able to get back to it right away, skipping over stress and frustration is a powerful exercise on its own.

A good example of when patience came in handy was the time I took my car to get a new headlight. When I pulled into the service station, I parked in the entrance to one of the bays where the mechanics work on the cars. There was one car ahead of me. A car which had finished being worked on in another bay pulled away, so I decided to try to pull out of my space and pull into the entrance of the now empty bay. Presently, a FedEx truck arrived and parked behind me so I couldn't back out so I was forced to wait for the car in front of me to finish while the FedEx truck behind me unloaded a bunch of large boxes. When the car in my bay drove away and I finally pulled in, the mechanic searched for my replacement bulb and told me the shop didn't have the one I needed. Then he stopped and thought for a moment, and opened one of the boxes the FedEx driver had unloaded. He pulled out the bulb I needed from the box and installed it in my car. In that situation, if I had arrived any earlier or not been impeded by the FedEx truck, I probably wouldn't have gotten the bulb I needed. The situation called for me to sit and wait patiently so that the truck could unload the bulb that the shop did not have in stock. Any annoyance I felt was resistance to the very situation that was "trying" to help me.

Whenever you go someplace, take your mind off yourself. Instead, be curious about what's going on there. What are the people around you trying to achieve? How can you be of service to them? Try to be helpful and inquisitive wherever you go, even if you're a customer and someone is serving you. Get a feel for the energy of the place at that time. Do the people seem happy to be there? If you show up someplace and start being helpful in an unobtrusive way, it will change the mood of everyone there and they'll likely start being helpful too. As you're guiding yourself through your daily life, don't push your agenda on others. You must be aware of the energetic quality of your environment and determine the level of receptivity of the situation to your agenda. Pay attention to the environment around you and determine what it calls for or what it's allowing. Recognize how you're feeling and what your agenda is. Personal pacing means going with the flow of a situation unless it has a bad energy. While it's important for you to focus on achieving your goals for the day, recognize that sometimes some will be left undone and others may resolve in different ways than you expected. I used to get angry when I was driving and I got lost or took a wrong turn. Sometimes, what seems like an unwanted detour can turn out to be advantageous. Maybe the universe is gently steering you in a new direction for some reason unknown until later.

Your agenda is an energy, and people receptive to it will go with it, but only if they're allowed to do so on their own terms. No one likes the hard sell; just "show and let go." People's intentions are notoriously difficult to anticipate, especially when they haven't yet made up their minds. Don't cringe or become defensive as soon as someone criticizes you. It may mean they're trying to buy into your agenda but are fighting their own personal barriers. People who are ready to say yes often employ a strategy of criticism or doubt to create a "symbolic resistance" designed to put up enough of a front in order that they don't appear as a pushover. This calls for calm and gentle reassurance; don't overplay your hand. People do things for their reasons, not yours. Give people the time they need to allow your ideas to feel comfortable enough to fit into their agendas. Watch for examples of this in your daily life and notice instances when someone originally resistant to an idea warms up to it. Try to find out what clarified the person's understanding or made him change his mind.

Personal pacing means living your daily life in tune with your environment and having an awareness that operates at a higher level than your current agenda. It's possible that your agenda isn't right for your current audience and that it may not even be right for you, but you don't realize it. You have to judge if the "no" responses you keep getting are just stepping stones to success or if they mean you need to reevaluate your agenda or your presentation of it. The best products and services tend to sell themselves. If you have to push too hard, either your approach is offensive or what you're proposing isn't of value to that particular audience. Make sure your agenda or your product or service has the right intentions behind it. If you're able to accept, rather than resist the current moment, you'll have the detached perspective necessary to make it work best for you.

Chapter 4 Exercises

Exercise 1. Personality Evaluation

Write a one-page description of your personality. Include how you interact with friends, coworkers, family, and strangers. Then take a few inexpensive personality tests at the library or online, and note the results. Ask several of your friends and coworkers to give you an honest evaluation of your personality as a "personal growth exercise." Get data from as many sources as you can to build an objective profile of yourself. Note how this profile compares to your original one-page description. Did any of your results surprise you or conflict with how you thought of yourself before? Some people are completely unaware that their behavior rubs others the wrong way. Could this be true for you? You may have behaviors that are selfish, offensive or otherwise off-putting that you aren't aware of. If you can uncover these behaviors, you can change them and change the way others react to you and improve your results.

Exercise 2. Practice Meeting New People

My wife, Amy, a naturally introverted person, is slow to meet new people. She's usually more comfortable interacting with people in her familiar social circle. Recently, she volunteered to manage the annual 10 kilometer race fundraiser for our children's school. She did a great job making all the arrangements, but I was particularly proud at how she persuaded business owners to donate thousands of dollars to the school. She overcame her trepidation and approached businesspeople wherever she went to ask for donations. I found her ability to approach new people surprising and inspiring considering her traditional reluctance.

Join a Meetup group or a Toastmasters club. Take some Dale Carnegie classes, join a sports group, or get a part-time job where you serve the public. Take the time to introduce yourself to everyone in the group and find out something about each person. If you can't fit room in your schedule, change your regular routine in some way so that you have the opportunity to meet new people and break the ice. If you frequent a coffee shop or grocery store, practice striking up a conversation with the other people standing in line. The easier that social interaction becomes with strangers, the more comfortable and confident you'll be in any situation. The easiest level of conversation with strangers is in exchanging pleasantries. The next level is engaging in more serious conversation like sharing stories or asking for advice. A more advanced level is anticipating what the person will find helpful or funny, and pleasantly surprising them.

Exercise 3. Turn Down Job Offers

Even if you're currently employed, happy with your job, and have no intention of leaving, apply for a few jobs for which you're qualified, just for the sake of getting the practice. If you get an interview, prepare for it by watching the job interview scene with Ben Affleck from the movie Good Will Hunting on YouTube a couple of times. That scene is a little over the top and I don't recommend you asking for an immediate cash retainer, but it's hilarious and can put you in a funny and confident mood. Have some interesting and funny job-related stories handy that you can share with the recruiters and interviewers. Take control of the interview by having pre-prepared materials to present. Explain to the hiring managers why you enjoy doing just the kind of work they're offering, highlighting specific examples. If you're offered the job and that company still hasn't convinced you to leave your current job, gracefully turn it down while retaining a good relationship with that prospective employer. You can even offer to do consulting work on the side for that company until they find the right candidate. I guarantee you that if you handle this situation smoothly, you'll come out feeling energized and even more confident in your current job. Gracefully turning down a job opportunity makes you feel that opportunities are plentiful for you, and that you, rather than jobs, are a scarce resource.

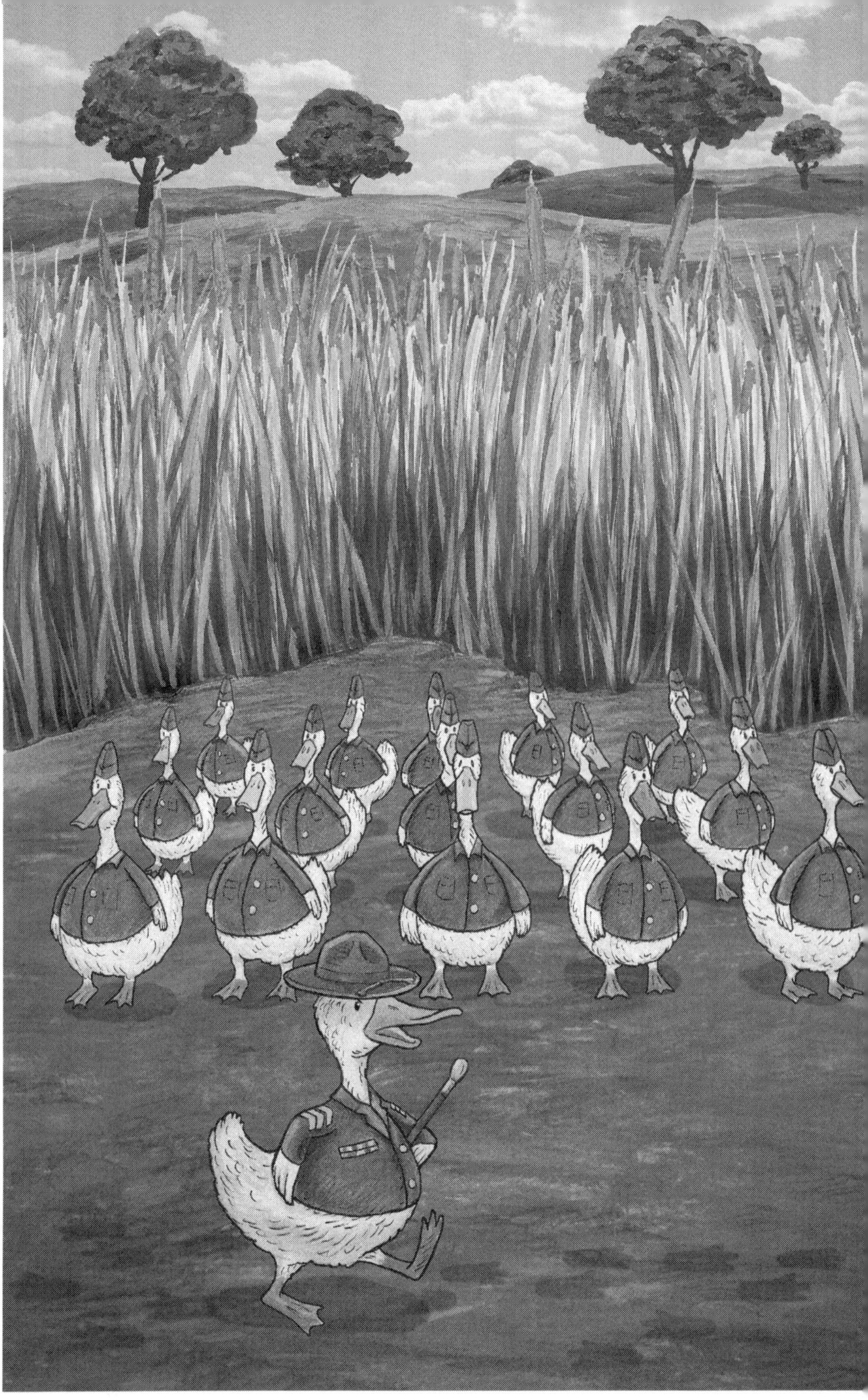

Chapter 5

Personal Inventory

The same high-quality thought you apply to your career should apply to every area of your life. It makes little sense to focus on your career to the detriment of your health, finances, or emotional outlook. If these other areas are optimized, they can contribute to your energy and facilitate your career progress. This seems so obvious as to not merit inclusion in this book. However, I can easily think of many examples of people whom I've worked with as well as famous personalities in many public arenas whose personal issues hold back their progress and ruin their reputations.

In this chapter, you will take a personal inventory of some major areas of your life to minimize any drag they may be having on your progress. We're going to visit your health, your attitude, your financial status, and your relationships. Each of these topics is huge, and entire industries exist to help you maximize their effectiveness. A comprehensive review of each is beyond the scope of this book and my abilities. I address them here primarily for you to keep in mind the importance each plays in your life and how they relate to your career. We're also going to take a look at the thoughts, beliefs, and decisions that got you to where you are today. I've found it helpful to compare "where my head was at" in the past with my major interests and concerns today.

Imagine you're a military commander sending an elite force of soldiers to fight the enemy. You would arm the soldiers with the best food, the best weapons, the best protective clothing, the best technology, and the best training possible. You ought to take your own life's challenges as seriously as a military strategist who's preparing to fight the enemy on the battlefield. You must equip yourself with the best possible diet, exercise, sleep, attitude, financial knowledge, and overall mindset. Give yourself every possible advantage. Don't send yourself out into the world unprepared.

Many people tend to overemphasize some areas and leave others lacking. For example, some exercise several times per week but have poor diets and smoke cigarettes or pay little attention to their finances. Others optimize their money but never exercise or have poor sleeping habits. It's not necessary to bench press 300 pounds or sleep ten hours a night, especially if other areas of your life are left unattended. Do justice to every area of your life. If you're over-optimizing one area you may be taking away energy from the others.

When my oldest son was three years old, I once asked him, "How is it that people exist?" He said, "Because of air!" I replied, "Where does the air come from?" He said, "It comes from their mouths!" I laughed while thinking about people producing air inside themselves and then breathing it out into the world from their mouths. Then I imagined that he may have been trying to explain that people were able to come into existence because favorable precursor conditions existed (the air). This implies that if you want to achieve some result, you don't necessarily have to make it happen by force. Rather, you may merely need to make the surrounding conditions right and allow the result to happen naturally. Your career exists against the backdrop of your health, attitude, finances, and relationships. Spend time carefully arranging these to ensure they support, rather than inhibit, your result coming to fruition. *Optimize every area of your life to support your goals.*

Health

How would you rate your current state of physical health today? You can't expect to perform at consistently high levels if your health is poor or mediocre. The easiest way to carry out any activity, especially ones which require high levels of perseverance and concentration over long periods of time, is to do so with a steady supply of high quality energy. Your body is designed to supply you with this energy and will do so indefinitely to the extent that you develop and lock in healthy living habits. Because people are creatures of habit and tend to their needs in much the same way every day, improving your health is simply a matter of adopting good habits and leaving behind any bad ones.

Sleep

My day doesn't begin when I wake up in the morning. For me, every day begins the night before. I know that if I avoid alcohol and go to bed early, I'll wake up on time, feeling great. If I drink alcohol or go to bed late, or both, I won't feel good when I wake up and I won't be as productive as I otherwise would have during the day. Sleep is absolutely critical to mood regulation and mental function. Do the best you can to keep a regular schedule and get to bed on time. Keep a pad and pen near your bed so you can write down any ideas you may happen to get in the middle of the night and then go back to sleep.

Some people feel guilty for pressing the snooze button when the alarm goes off. I've watched presentations where the speaker gives advice on how to get up early and start being productive even when you're still sleepy and would rather push the snooze button several times. I'm not a doctor, so I can't speak with authority on medical topics. However, both common sense and my personal experience dictate that if you still feel sleepy in the morning, it's because you're sleep-deprived and you need more sleep. Though this book focuses on careers, I value my health more than my career. If I still feel sleepy in the morning, I'd rather get an extra hour of sleep and arrive late at work than force myself to operate on inadequate sleep. My performance at work will be much better if I sleep in and come to work late than if I don't get the sleep I need. My jobs have usually been flexible where I can occasionally arrive and leave later than normal in order to be as effective as possible. If I had a job where I had to report to work at a specific hour, you can bet I would have a militaristic nighttime routine to make getting in bed on time a priority. Having young children who sometimes don't sleep well necessitates going to bed even earlier than normal to give myself enough leeway to still get enough sleep.

Sleep is even more important for me than diet or exercise because the negative effects are more immediate when I abuse my sleep. On just one night, if I get two hours less sleep than normal, I immediately feel awful. If I overeat or neglect to exercise for a week or two, it doesn't really change how I feel or perform right away. I once did a water fast for three days before a surgery. After not eating any food at all (except water) for three days, I felt just fine. (Don't try this at home without consulting a medical professional!) After the surgery, I had to go for two months without exercising while my body healed. When I finally started exercising again, I wasn't as strong as before, but I still felt great. If I go on vacation for a week and completely abandon my healthy diet, I still feel just fine even though I may gain a few pounds. However, whenever I fail to sleep properly on just one night, the effects are immediate, severe, and brutal. Most evenings, I strive to make it to bed by 9pm, and though I usually "fail", I still manage to get to bed by 10pm or 10:30, which is just fine. How I feel when I wake up makes a huge difference in how I perform during the day. Make good sleep one of your highest priorities.

Diet

Obesity rates in the U.S. have risen dramatically since the 1980s and it has become a major health problem. It's hard to believe but currently two thirds of Americans are considered overweight! To maintain a healthy weight, you need to scrutinize the composition and quantity of everything you eat. If you do so consistently, your body composition will hover around your most healthy weight. Each person's body and nutritional needs are different based on their size, activity level, and other factors. The primary reason anyone ever loses weight and keeps it off is that they maintain thoughtful attention to what they eat. It's like driving. Pay attention, get good results. Don't pay attention, get bad results. It's up to you to research, adopt, and maintain a diet which keeps your energy levels even throughout the day and minimizes spikes and troughs.

I used to love to overeat. I remember taking a date to a restaurant one evening for dinner. I ordered chicken but the waiter brought me a pork dish by mistake. By the time he brought my food I'd forgotten what I'd ordered and it didn't really matter to me. When I had eaten half my meal already, the waiter came to the table and apologized for giving me the wrong dish. I said it was no problem at all, but I requested he also bring me the chicken dish, and I ate that too. When my date was unsure about what she wanted for dessert, I just ordered multiple desserts and ate whatever she didn't want. I also remember a particular Christmas dinner at my in-laws' house. Everyone had finished their meal, left the table, and had gone to another room. Several people had left their plates on the table with a significant amount of uneaten food on the plates. I noticed this and promptly sat down at each of their places and ate all their leftovers! I must say that I was much heavier then than I am now.

There's a quote that says something like, "If you divided all the wealth in the world evenly among all the people, within a short while, all of the money would be right back where it started." I like that quote because it's referring to people's orientation towards money. Some people, no matter how much money they start out with, tend to spend too much and end up broke. Others invest and save lots of money over time, no matter how little they started with. That same principle also applies to weight. If you could snap your fingers and magically set everyone to their ideal weight, within a short while, everyone would end up back where they started. To stay lean, you need to change your relationship with food or your bad habits will regain control. This reminds me of the quote by Richard Bach, "If you love someone, set them free." My version of that is "If you hate your extra fat, set your bad habits free. If the fat comes back to you, your bad habits never really left."

My better judgment and my physiological dietary urges are still involved in a never-ending battle. My willpower waxes and wanes but these urges never take a vacation because they were designed by mother nature to keep us alive. Whenever I succumb to these urges, whatever weight loss progress I may have made throughout the day is lost and I have to start over the next day. To add insult to injury, I don't sleep well after drinking alcohol so it makes for a less-than-optimal day after. Through experimentation, I found I could "whittle down my weaknesses" to the most bare essentials. I used to regularly eat cookies most evenings after dinnertime along with two or three alcoholic drinks. When I first started to clean up my diet, I replaced the cookies with natural peanut butter (no added sugar) and low-sugar dark chocolate. Then I decided to limit alcohol to two drinks per day. I realized I didn't miss the cookies or extra alcohol. Then I reduced the alcohol to one drink per day and decided to reserve the peanut butter and chocolate to three or four times per week rather than every day. Sometimes I eat the peanut butter without the chocolate. Over time I realized how good I feel in the morning without drinking any alcohol and I now reserve it only for special occasions. If you gradually wean yourself from your weaknesses, over time they'll reach more acceptable levels in tune with a healthy lifestyle.

Some diet gurus say you can eat as much as you want of certain macronutrient groups without gaining weight. Not only is this not true in my experience, it's not the proper spiritual perspective on the subject. For me, portion size is key to weight maintenance. There is nothing more sensible than good old-fashioned moderation. The notion that it's somehow okay to practice regular gluttony in some areas of your life is a slippery slope towards making dysfunction the norm. Part of building character is embracing certain limits on one's urges and drives. It's unhealthy to think you can or should have everything you want, as much as you want, all the time. It may be helpful to remind yourself at each meal that you'll be eating again soon so there's no need to overdo it on the portion sizes.

The most important ingredient in your diet is thought. How much thought do you put into what you eat each day? Lots of people lose weight on vastly different diet plans because they all contain more thought than no plan at all. You ought to examine what and how much you're eating and make sure it's supporting your healthiest self. I'm not a dietician so I can't prescribe or proscribe any particular eating plan for anyone. What I can do is tell you what works for me. I maintain a healthy weight when I do the following.

- Reserve sugar and alcohol only for special occasions.

- Avoid white flour, pasta, and overly processed foods..
- Eat sensible portion sizes.
- Balance protein, fat, and healthy carbohydrates at every meal.

I do indulge in sugar, alcohol, pizza, and other vices, but (usually) only on special occasions. I celebrate specific pre-determined special occasions each year which include holidays, birthdays, vacations, and family events. I know what these are in advance and I usually don't deviate from my diet rules except for during these times. Some people benefit from the use of weekly "cheat days" or "cheat meals" but those haven't worked for me. I have enough slip-ups in my weekly eating that any sort of scheduled cheating would be counterproductive. The following is what I tell myself to help me keep on track. "Don't mess up your special occasions by not eating everything you'd like. Don't mess up the rest of the time by eating things you know you shouldn't." Shun all non-essential food when it's not a special occasion.

Exercise

Adopting a regular exercise routine can raise your energy levels and improve how you look and feel. Exercise has tremendous benefits for health and longevity. I find it helpful to perform a variety of exercise to keep it fun and interesting and to challenge my mind and body in different ways. I do yoga, weights, jump rope, running and roller skating. I take my kids to the park and use the opportunity to exercise on the equipment there. I also take them to an indoor trampoline park and exercise there too. I keep exercise clothes and shoes in my car so I'm always ready to get a workout in if the opportunity presents itself.

When it comes to exercise, I see too many people at the extremes. It seems to me that most people either don't exercise at all or overdo it. Treat your body with care and respect and it will serve you into your golden years. The goal of exercising is to improve your overall health. There's no point in it if you over-train or injure yourself. Frequency and intensity of exercise should be inversely proportional. For example, if you exercise with high intensity, you should probably do so with low frequency to let your body recover. If you only do low-impact exercise, like walking or water aerobics, you should probably exercise several days per week. The exercise I do is of moderate intensity so I exercise between two and four days per week. I keep a poster-sized twelve-month calendar in my garage where I note what exercise I did on a specific date. If I lift weights one day, I'll probably do something different for the next couple of workouts before I return to weights to let myself recover. I try to cycle through my different exercise routines in order to keep it fun and maximize my recovery.

The world can sometimes be chaotic, challenging, and dangerous. Making your health and fitness one of your top priorities will best position you to handle life's inevitable challenges.

Attitude

Most essays on improving attitude focus on encouraging readers to cultivate a feeling of thankfulness for their current circumstances, family, living situation, financial standing, etc. If you are upset because you were just fired or laid off, or if you're a new entrant into the workforce with few ideas of how to start, or if you're stuck in a job you hate, mustering feelings of gratitude may not feel authentic. Expecting you to feel genuine enthusiasm under these circumstances is just too much to ask and would constitute impractical, if not disingenuous, advice. Having said that, it's important to understand that any negative thoughts you have about your current reality are a form of suffering. If you ask yourself questions like "Why do others have so much money and luck and I don't?" or "What's wrong with me?" your mind will respond by providing discouraging answers. Do not resist the truth of your current reality.

The creative, energized mindset is the one most likely to lead you to success, and the first step to getting there is to fully accept and make peace with your current circumstances. You don't have to feign happiness for your circumstances if you can't muster it. It's not necessary. Just adopt a mindset where negative emotions associated with your present condition are allowed to dissipate and leave a sense of peace and acceptance in their place. When your psyche is bogged down by negative thoughts and feelings, everyone around you immediately picks up on this negativity and it taints their enthusiasm for you and limits your opportunities.

Acceptance is liberating because it means you're ready to start anew, unencumbered by negativity. You don't have to feel anything you don't want to; all you have to do is allow your current circumstances to be what they are. Detaching your feelings of suffering and anxiety from your current circumstances starts with the realization that your circumstances and your feelings about them are two separate things, and that they're both temporary. Your circumstances right now are what they are. It's up to you whether to continue suffering or allow the negativity to dissipate. The following Ralph Waldo Emerson quote has helped me through quite a few difficult instances. "Finish each day and be done with it. You have done what you could. Some blunders and absurdities no doubt crept in; forget them as soon as you can. Tomorrow is a new day. You shall begin it serenely and with too high a spirit to be encumbered with your old nonsense."

In contrast to acceptance, thankfulness represents a genuine contentment with your situation and is more potent. The attitude of thankfulness puts you in a position of power. You're telling the world that you're perfectly content with what you have right now and that whatever pursuits you're currently doing are icing on the cake that you're both having and eating. Thankfulness gives you confidence because you're acknowledging the abundance that already exists for you now, and that confidence leads to more abundance. I'm not pushing you to feel thankful, I'm just advertising it.

Finances

Whatever your financial situation is right now, it's imperative that you understand it thoroughly. Evaluate how much debt you have, to whom, and the interest rate for each obligation. Do you have to make monthly payments right now on all the debt or are there some debts which can be suspended, like certain college loans? Understand what assets you have and the value and liquidity of each. Compare your current monthly income after taxes with your monthly expenses for the past two months. Are there times during the month when you regularly run out of money? Identify superfluous expenses that you can avoid next month and trends in your spending which can be improved. Cultivating a lifestyle that's inexpensive to maintain will give you more options and elongate the period you can maintain your lifestyle without working. You'll have less stress and more confidence knowing that you're not completely beholden to a paycheck from your employer. Stress related to personal finances can hamper your career progress because it puts a strain on your creative energies and points you towards areas where money is the primary goal rather than providing value for others.

Always think first before you spend money, especially on large items. Consider if you can do without whatever might be captivating your interest right now, or postpone your decision for later. Several years ago my swimming pool was cracked inside and the concrete around the pool was in disrepair. Because I had the funds available, I spent $10,000 to completely re-do the pool and buy new filter equipment, etc. Two years later, I decided I didn't want the pool anymore because my in-laws down the street had a pool and it cost me too much to maintain ours. So I spent another $5,000 to have the pool removed! If I'd taken the time to really understand my feelings about the pool, I would have removed it rather than fixed it, and I'd have that $10,000 in the bank right now. That has to be one of the dumbest financial mistakes I've ever made, and the thought of it still causes me to feel shame. The only upside is that the pain from that awful decision helps to ensure I make better decisions in the future.

Once you've done an inventory of your current wealth, accept that it is your present financial reality. Also accept that you can improve upon this reality and start making smarter decisions about what you do with the money that flows to you. Whether people know it or not, everyone has a specific orientation towards money. Many people can't help but spend every penny they receive, often on unnecessary things. Other people save all their money and reserve little for their enjoyment. Both of these orientations are dysfunctional. Everyone comes in contact with money almost every day and makes choices about what they're going to do with it. My purpose here isn't to teach you about personal finance. Rather, it's to stress its importance to your success. Well-informed people with good money habits tend to accumulate more money over time. Most everybody else ends up with insufficient funds. Libraries, bookstores, and the internet are chock full of excellent financial advice for people in every situation. Now is the time to learn what you need to learn and do what you need to do to build your financial security. Make sure this gets on your radar and informs what you do with your money each day.

Relationships

The people with whom you spend the most time have the most influence on your mood, attitudes, and mindset. To cultivate and maintain the positive mindset you need over long periods of time, you have to take a hard look at those closest to you and determine if their continuing influence in your life is healthy and beneficial. Do you have relationships that should end or be allowed to fade away? This may free up much-needed time and energy. Are there people who bring you down but whom you keep in your life anyway? If so, I challenge you to be the one who sets the tone of the relationship. Find out which areas of their life are sapping their energy and help them make their own improvements. Rather than letting them bring you down with their negative vibes, you bring them up to your level. Let your happiness and positivity counteract their gloomy crabbiness. Let them know you only have time and patience for people who are headed in a positive direction.

One of the hallmarks of being a mature adult is the ability to have difficult conversations. Many people avoid conflict because they fear other people's reactions or they fear they'll be judged as hostile or difficult. This fear holds them back because they fail to stand up for themselves in important situations. I have a friend who had negotiated a bonus and a raise once he had reached certain milestones in his job. After he'd fully accomplished those, the company was dragging its heels when it came to paying his bonus and raise. Sometimes we'd go to coffee and he'd complain about not getting what was promised to him. Multiple times I encouraged him to have a serious discussion with his boss and hold the company accountable, but to my knowledge, he never did. His excuse was that he liked his job, didn't want to make waves, and felt he was already fairly compensated. I found this very frustrating because I knew his inability to stand up for himself would be interpreted as weakness and hamper his ability to further negotiate with his superiors.

I once had a boss who was both intelligent and disagreeable. I genuinely admired his wisdom and personality when he was in a good mood, which, sadly, was quite rare. His behavior was often offensive to me and to many other people in the office. It reached such a difficult point that whenever this person would cross the line, I would keep a record of the specifics of the incident. After documenting a few incidents, I had a meeting with him in his office. Even though he was the boss, I felt compelled to address his numerous offenses. I structured my remarks so that they were very specific. I said, "On (such and such date) you said (such and such remark) to (such and such person)." I continued, "Not only was this offensive to everyone present, it caused me to have to spend thirty minutes counseling (such and such person) who was crying after the incident." Although he walked out of the office in an emotional state, he later sent me an email thanking me for my feedback. Standing up for myself and others made a big difference in how I felt about my workplace. After giving occasionally crabby people the benefit of the doubt when appropriate, I will always stand up for myself and others when it becomes necessary. I would even coach the CEO of a corporation in this same way if he or she acted inappropriately with zero fear of being fired because I refuse to be mistreated in the workplace.

When you're at work, beware of people who love Fridays and hate Mondays or use the phrases "hump day," "same stuff different day," or "same old same old". By using these phrases, they're telling you that they feel like helpless victims of circumstance who have little control over their fate. They're saying they dislike Mondays as if they're compelled by some nonspecific malevolent force to attend work every day. These are the same people who would immediately quit their jobs if they had enough money to sustain themselves without working. Their bosses are keenly aware of their attitudes so these people usually aren't well paid and get passed up for promotions. Start associating with successful people around you; find out what motivates them, how they think and operate, and how they succeeded. The goal of this book is to help you transcend dissatisfaction with your professional life to happily working on projects you enjoy which build skills you truly value. The person who can make this shift in mindset approaches his life thoughtfully and doesn't experience weekly elation and depression related to leaving and returning to work. Be honest with yourself if you have the Sunday night blues and do something about it. Wherever you go, relate with people in ways that increase everyone's happiness and vibrancy while avoiding people with low or negative energy

Decisions

Excessive brooding over the past certainly isn't helpful for advancing your career. However, it can be an enlightening exercise to examine the progression of your thought processes starting at a meaningful point in the past, up through today. What was most important to you five or ten years ago? What were you focusing on back then? How did your emphasis on that topic influence where you are today? In recent years, my focus has changed from self-motivation and advancement in my twenties and early thirties to emphasis on managing a successful family and work life balance in my forties. I know this may sound ridiculous, but I have often criticized myself for not taking seriously in the past things which only became important to me more recently. Take investing for retirement for example. In my twenties and early thirties my investment strategy was uninformed and haphazard. I've often kicked myself for not getting much more serious much earlier. To get through this, it helped me to identify why my mindset was what it was, to forgive myself, to move past any feelings of frustration, and to start over. Because I understand what I was thinking ten years ago, I no longer judge my past self based on my current priorities.

The thought experiment of going back in time and giving your past self advice can be fun and interesting. What I've found, however, is that the advice you would give yourself tends only to pertain to the priorities you have at the time you perform the experiment. For example, a man in his twenties might tell his teenage self to be more fearless when talking to girls. That same man in his thirties might tell his twenties self to start saving money, avoid frivolous purchases, and take more risks in his career. The same man in his 50s may tell his younger self to spend more time with his family and children. How well do you understand how you got to where you are today and why? Are you pleased with the life decisions you've made so far? If not, can you make peace with them and start over? Consider what yourself ten years from now would like to tell yourself today. What priorities will you have then for which you can start preparing now?

How you got to where you are today is the accumulation of decisions you've made in your life, both big and small, good and bad. If you have some good habits and some bad habits, your accumulated result will be a mediocre mixture of the good and bad. Every day people make thousands of decisions about what to do and each decision has consequences. Every time you make a good decision, it's like depositing money into a bank account. Whenever you make a bad decision, it's like a withdrawal from that bank account, or inflicting some wound upon yourself, depending on the magnitude of the bad decision. The consequences of these decisions add up over time and result in your current condition. People who lead unsatisfying lives do so because their result is the combined outcome of more bad decisions than good. Morally speaking, there's no such thing as a right or wrong decision as long as you're not hurting anyone. However, many decisions are better than others based on your own personal value system. If you make better decisions, you'll end up with better results, and vice versa.

Good decisions are almost always harder to make than bad ones. That's because the best version of yourself requires higher quality thought and more energy than some other version. Picking the right type and amount of food to eat takes more energy and effort than eating as much as you want of whatever is available. Study and exercise take energy, time, and concerted effort. Getting to bed on time requires attention to what time it is and to maneuvering through the obstacles between you and getting to bed early. With most decisions, you usually know which ones you *should* choose but you often do what you feel like doing. The trouble with relying on what you feel like doing is that if you haven't already been following a good plan for your sleep, diet, exercise, and attitude, you'll have low energy and you wont feel like making the better decisions. If you adopt healthy habits in each area of your life, the better choices will take less willpower. I once read that willpower is a limited resource and decreases throughout the day. It took months for me to get out of the habit of after-dinner alcoholic drinks and dessert. Now that I only eat dessert on special occasions, I don't have to think about whether I have treats after dinner. I just follow my plan.

Evaluate the feelings that you associate with your current daily activities and ask yourself, "Does doing this thing make me feel like I'm doing something good for myself and others?" "Do my current pursuits feel like the right thing for me right now?" and "Am I filled with excitement to get up every day and make more progress?" Take time to recall how you got to where you are today. Recall the real reasons why you made your past decisions and make peace with those. Doing so will let you keep the past in the past and keep your focus on the now, where it should be. The past is the past and you must make peace with it if you intend to move forward with a light, happy heart.

Chapter 5 Exercises

Exercise 1. Take better care of yourself.

Develop a simple written outline for how you are going to take care of yourself in the areas of health, attitude, finances, and relationships. For each area, write a few bullet points about how you're going to improve your corresponding habits. Consider what habits the best version of you would adopt. It might look something like this:

Health
   Get to bed each night by 10pm.
   Substitute herbal tea for soda.
   Eat dessert only on special occasions.

Attitude
   Complement three people per day on something positive they did or said.
   Take a five-minute meditation break every day after lunch.
   Offer to help at least one person per day with any task.

Finances
   Start investing in the 401k at work.
   Meet with a financial counselor at the bank to begin debt consolidation.
   Limit eating out to once per week.

Relationships
   Stop spending time with [person x] after work and go to the gym instead.
   Stop lending money to [person y].
   Talk with [person z] about boundaries.

Exercise 2. Which of your possessions would you re-buy?

Slowly walk around your house or apartment, from room to room, and look at your various possessions. While looking at each one, ask yourself these two questions:

1. "If I did not have this possession right now and instead I had the money back that it cost, would I soon go out and re-buy it?"

2. "Did I really need this possession at the time I bought it?"

You'll probably realize that you wasted quite a bit of money. Consider selling or giving away the items which no longer serve you or represent your interests or values. Ridding your life of unnecessary possessions can feel cathartic. Clean and arrange your living space to maximize your creativity and productivity. You can do the same with friends, social networking contacts, investments, clothes, books, food items etc. Surround yourself only with people and things which support your vision of your best self.

Exercise 3. Secret Camera Crew

What would you learn about yourself if a secret camera crew created a 3-hour-long documentary of the past ten years of your life and showed it to you? What themes would emerge about your behavior that you'd want to change or improve right away? Can you think back to various points in your past and remember what your priorities were at those times? The progression of your motives over time may seem blurry and jumbled, elusive to your grasp. To get a clearer picture of your specific priorities in the past, identify three or four people who've known you well for quite a long time. Have a talk with each of them about what they remember regarding your priorities and focus in the past, and write them down. Adopt a non-judgmental point of view and accept that this is the impression they had of you. Once you've collected their responses, identify common themes and reflect on the person they are describing. If this exercise helps you more clearly identify your motives and priorities in the past, it will be easier for you to sympathize with your former self and understand why you are where you are today.

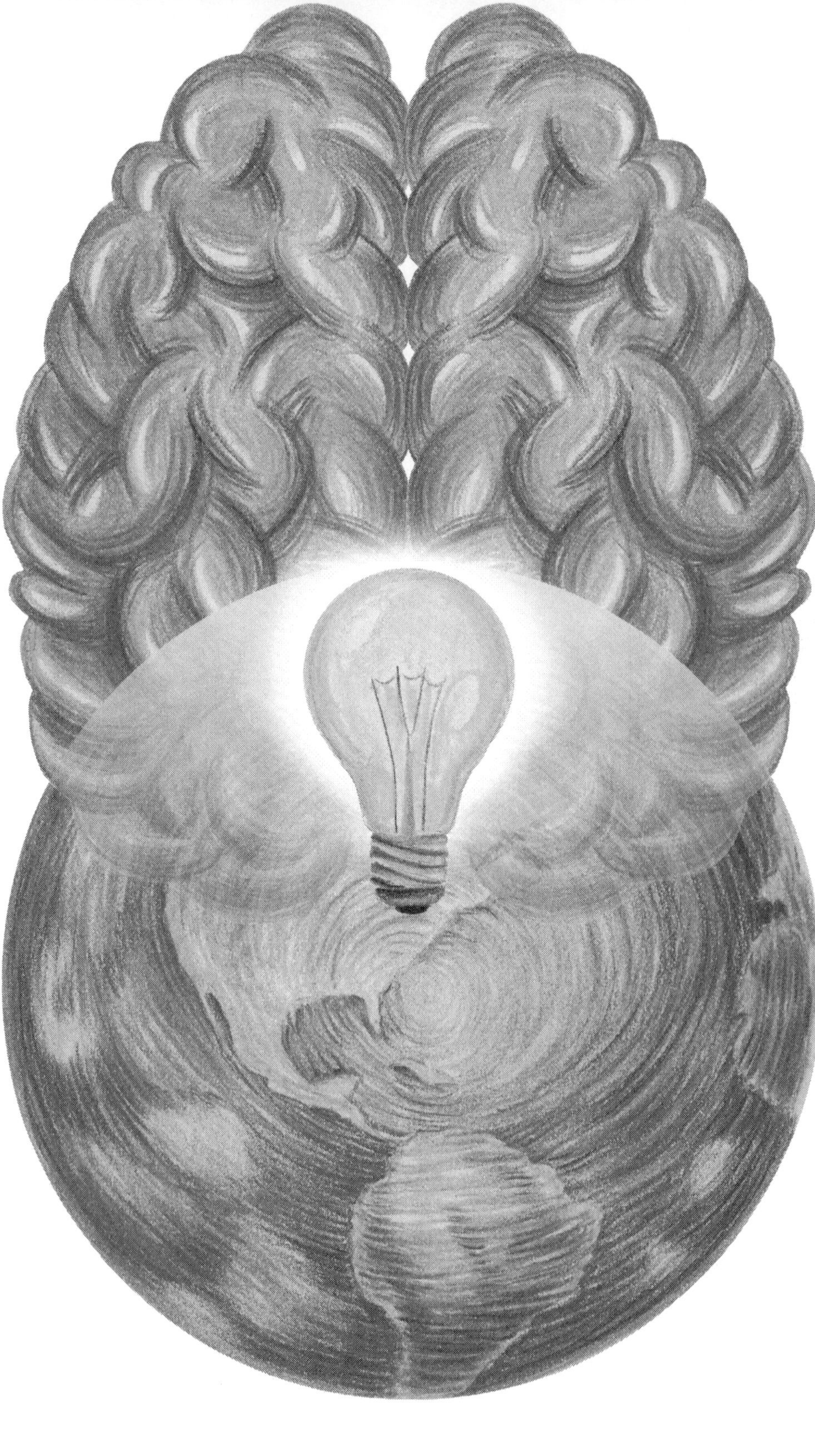

Chapter 6

Identify Your Interests

How well have you identified your professional goals? Do you know exactly what you want to pursue? Some people dance around these questions and fail to identify specific answers for themselves. How would you know that an answer you thought of is the right answer? There are many right answers for you and what they all have in common is that they make you feel excited to get up in the morning and take steps toward your goal. They also make you feel pride in your skills and an urgency to continue improving.

So why might you have trouble identifying what to pursue? Perhaps you rarely think about it with the intent of coming up with a concrete answer upon which you would then take action. Maybe you already have ideas about what you want, but you assume that it's unrealistic for you or that becoming capable and qualified would take too much effort. You may have only one or two primary skills or interests right now or you may have a wide variety of different skills and interests. Do you just randomly choose one? Do you choose your favorite? Do you choose the one that has the potential of making the most money or helping the most people? Do you try to combine one or more of them? What if you don't know "what you love" or you can't identify a career-related interest? I imagine many people fall into this category. You know that just getting any old job may not lead to fulfillment. You have much intelligence, interest, and enthusiasm, but maybe you're not sure how or where to apply these. This chapter will help you explore your personal interests from different angles and encourage you to identify some which can be candidates for work-related pursuits. The practical way to move forward in your career is to *develop and refine your interests through exposure, experience, and trial and error.*

How Do You Know If Something Is Right for You?

At the beginning of my career my dad took me to visit a family friend for career advice. I told him I'd studied accounting but wanted to get into other areas. He told me I should stick to what I studied and "pay my dues" before looking elsewhere. I was told I needed to have a "burning desire" to succeed. I didn't take his advice. Instead, I went back to school and studied marketing which expanded my options. I then got a job in a company's marketing department using databases to create automated marketing reports. I found this work to be challenging, stimulating, and fun. This ultimately led to my career in what was then a new field called "business intelligence." Any worthwhile pursuit which brings significant value to other people takes a lot of energy to accomplish. Focusing on things which bring you joy will point you towards areas which will interest you enough to allow you to muster this high level of energy needed. If you enjoy something enough to stick with it through the inevitable bumps, pitfalls, and difficulties, you'll eventually make progress and gain expertise.

Joy sustains itself naturally while burning desire is a fire that must be constantly stoked, tended, and fed new fuel. The fuel of most burning desires is the fuel of the ego. Joy is more enduring than ego because it's based on real pleasure rather than on wanting or striving. Adequate exposure and self-exploration are so important because when you discover an interest which truly stimulates your enthusiasm, your work feels natural and doesn't require so much impassioned striving. A little healthy excitement each day is enough to keep you going.

"Do what you love and the money will follow." If you have financial commitments, you may not be able to just quit your job right away and dive into something you love. Depending on its value to society, the money may not follow! At least not right away. I believe you can monetize what you love but it may take longer than you'd like. I suggest starting small - in your garage like several successful companies have. You may stay in the garage until you've got enough revenue to make it out of the garage. But it's fine if it stays in the garage. Part of finding the right career is blending what you love with what society values and will pay for. The less society values what you love, the longer it will take to monetize your interest. If there isn't a straightforward link between your passion and a way to make a living, you'll need to develop a detailed plan for how you're going to monetize it, or at least how you'll continue without it creating a long term negative cash flow. You'll need to have the necessary patience to take it to the next level. Today's internet technology and social media can help you find your tribe and discover other people also interested in what you love.

I've talked about the idea of delivering value in exchange for the things you need and want. Well, in this book, I have to do more than just write motivational-sounding phrases like "If anyone can do it, you can do it!", "Follow your passion!" or "Never give up!" I need to deliver real value if I expect to make any substantive change in your life. I've seen presentations which ask short, introspective questions about what's most important to you. They ask what you are qualified to teach others and then declare, "That's your passion!" Personality test style career quizzes yield interesting findings but rarely deliver visceral feelings of certainty. While these approaches are a step closer to the right direction than general motivational phrases, they still only represent a small part of the solution. This is because it's impossible to determine something as important and elusive as your career choices through introspection alone. No amount of pure contemplation can produce worthwhile definitive answers. Anyone telling you that you can determine your career choice through mental exercises alone either doesn't fully understand the process or is trying to sell you something.

If that's true, then what advice does make sense? For you to obtain a high level of certainty about a particular career path, you must go way beyond just contemplating or scratching the surface of activities that come to mind. It's going to take a lot of legwork on your part! This process will at least take a number of months if not a year or more. You must obtain enough exposure and experience in areas you're considering to have enough information to confidently rule them in or out. There's no quick and easy way to make the right decisions for yourself that a book could provide. You can't find out that information on the internet. You don't know how you're going to feel about something until you actually do it. It's likely you'll end up surprising yourself. You have to go to where that activity is happening, see other people doing it, do it yourself, personally feel the pros and cons, get tired of it at the end of the day, do it some more the next day, gain a little bit of competency, and really get your hands dirty. In fact, I want you to get your whole arms and legs dirty!

While you're defining career paths for yourself, always remain suspicious that your decisions may be influenced by the insidious combination of lazy thinking and ego enhancement. These two factors together can plague people who haven't done enough work to better understand the most creative and productive paths for themselves. Because the self-discovery process is hard work, some people let lazy thinking take over and just settle on what they're already familiar with or what other people expect from them. They fail to make a specific enough plan for themselves and end up becoming part of someone else's plan. Later, when they realize they'd like to advance in their careers, they let their ego, rather than their creativity, be their guide. Because they haven't put in the time to develop better alternatives, they conclude that their current path is the right one and that the only direction to go is up. They make it their goal to be promoted to higher levels of authority and responsibility although they may be better suited elsewhere. They rationalize this notion using the increased salary and power they would gain in higher positions, because this appeals to their ego. When someone is promoted beyond their level of competency, it quickly becomes obvious to everyone in the workplace. Make sure the path you forge is the right one for you for the right reasons.

You'll know something you've discovered is right for you because it will stimulate feelings of excitement in you. It will engage your creativity, energy, and industry. It will consume your attention and you'll want to continue working to perfect it. You'll be inside of a positive feedback loop in which you perform the activity, get encouraging results, and gain more enthusiasm based on those results. You'll be proud of your finished work and take pride in it while you're doing it. Everyone has an "engine of productivity" inside them. It's just a matter of finding out exactly what it is and turning it on.

Sometimes when my children need money to buy something they want, they ask me if there are any chores they can do around the house to earn some money. Instead of identifying something specific, I ask them to walk around and "diagnose" what chores need to be done and then suggest how much money I should pay them for each job. This gives them the chance to be creative and decide for themselves what is needed. They do their own cost/benefit analysis based on their perceived level of effort to complete the chores. It's fun to watch them come up with ideas and then bargain with them for the price. They're usually very creative and come up with ideas I hadn't thought of. No one can or should decide for you what career to pursue. It's up to you to "diagnose" your communities and determine what's needed. This puts you in the driver's seat and lets you decide for yourself your preferred way to help.

If you're a recent college grad or early in your career, you may not have many skills you're uniquely good at that you can apply in a job. What you studied in school may be totally different when you find it in the real world. I got a bachelor's degree in accounting and passed the CPA exam before I realized I didn't want to be an accountant. I enjoyed the study of accounting, but not the practice. It took actually working in that field through a series of temp jobs before I found that out. You can't lose weight just by reading a book. You can't increase your physical fitness just by studying it in school. You have to do the exercises yourself! If you do the exercises in this book, I promise you'll be closer to determining your career than you are today.

The Chicken or the Egg

To increase your level of certainty about your areas of interest, you need to get sufficient exposure to many activities and opportunities, adequately evaluate your interest in them, and then refine and recalibrate your plan based on this newly integrated information. This process should be repeated until you've fine-tuned your unique way of adding value. This will allow you to learn things you didn't know before as well as clarify or correct your previous assumptions about a subject. You may currently be ruling out areas of interest which you'd greatly enjoy if you were to move beyond incorrect assumptions you've held about them. You'll know you've found the sweet spot when you're doing something:

- You enjoy
- You're good at
- That provides high value to others

This idea sounds simple but can be tricky if the activity which provides high value is difficult to master. Studies show that your affinity for something is directly related to your competency. The better you perform at something, the more you like it. For example, both roller skating and computer programming are difficult to do well and not nearly as much fun when you're a beginner. If I could snap my fingers and magically make you into an expert roller-skater or computer programmer, I guarantee you would love them, despite how you might feel about them today. However, the reality is that you have to endure a lengthy period of learning and struggling before you develop the competency that will allow you to fully enjoy the activity. The truly hard part happens when you're struggling and considering giving up. You become faced with the classic "chicken or egg" dilemma. It looks like this:

- Enjoyment depends on skill.
- Skill comes from hard work.
- Hard work is best motivated by enjoyment.

Enjoyment → Hard Work → Skill ↻

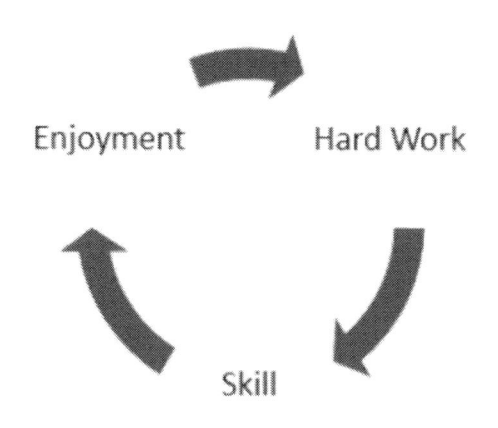

How does anyone break into this cycle if they don't already like something or are not already good at something? It's natural to ask yourself questions like, "Do I really like this enough to invest my time and energy learning it?", "If I keep going, will I ever master it?" and "If I do get good at this, will it pay off?" Only you can answer these questions for yourself. You must determine whether doing the activity is more fun than how hard it is to learn. I was still living at my parents' house in my early twenties when I decided to learn to play piano. I bought a cheap, used electric piano and a basic piano instruction book, and sat down to perform the exercises from the book. I followed the exercises for a couple of weeks but realized just how difficult piano is. I then changed my goal to learn *about* piano, practiced a couple more days and then stopped. I imagine playing piano is wonderful but, at that time, I decided it was harder to learn for me than how fun it was. Years later, I spent three years learning and practicing the oboe, and then gave that up once I had progressed to the skill level where I "shouldn't quit my day job." It's been a musical and occasionally melodious journey.

Consider whether you merely admire a topic or if you have a true interest. Someone who admires a particular activity may have learned about it and have some skills, but doesn't actively practice it and has few if any current goals in that area. Someone genuinely interested in something, however, practices it regularly, has plans to do it in the near future, has goals he is working towards, and doesn't anticipate quitting the activity anytime soon. He might even occasionally sacrifice sleep and skip meals doing this activity. Real interest drives consistent action. What do you intend to continue doing consistently? Through lots of direct exposure to a topic and achieving small milestones and successes you'll determine if it's right for you to keep going. You've got to get enough exposure to get past the introductory awkwardness and correctly rule it in our out. If you quit too soon, you may be ruling out something that could turn into a real passion.

In the next section, I present a four-step process you can follow to help organize your thoughts and get started in a good direction towards productive work. You can do this by yourself or with friends, and repeat this process to continue to refine your ideas.

Four-Step Work Identification Process

It can be challenging to organize your interests, feelings and the feedback from your work experiences in a way which allows you to process all the information together as a whole and make new decisions. I've developed a four-step process you can use to get your ideas on paper and study them more objectively. Feel free to make any changes necessary to make this work better for you.

Step 1: Lists

Get a large piece of paper, perhaps 18 inches tall by 24 inches wide. In landscape orientation, from left to right, write a set of lists containing several items each, in the following categories:

- Activities and personal interests I enjoy which give me feelings of fulfillment
- Skills in which I am currently proficient
- Skills and knowledge I would like to acquire
- Goods, services, and ideas I would like to see developed or improved
- Fulfilling ways I have helped others in the past

In addition to the above lists, you can create new categories of lists which resonate with you.

Step 2: Grouping

Get a set of crayons, colored pencils, or markers. Scan through all the items in every list. Starting with one color, circle items from the various lists which you feel may work synergistically to create a productive and fulfilling experience or activity. When you're done with one color, switch to another color to group other sets of items together. Continue this until you have at least three different colored groups of circled items. Some items may be circled in multiple colors.

Collectively, what do the items in each color group suggest to you? What themes do they represent? An example of a group of items circled in one color might include: "helping people solve problems," "writing fiction stories," "AutoCAD," "web design," "increased personalization of services" and "helped my nephew's 3rd grade class paint designs on his teacher's car". These items taken together may suggest many career options such as being an interior designer, writing articles for style and living magazines, developing floor plan software, writing children's books, opening a public art gallery, or developing your own lines of furniture and home decor items. The same group of ideas will have different meanings for each person. For each group, determine its primary significance to you in terms of some productive activity you could begin.

Step 3: Take action

Now choose one or two of your most appealing groups and act on the ideas you've developed. Based on what you choose, you have many possible options. Here is a list of things you can consider to get started:

Enroll in a class.
Write a business plan.
Do web or library research.
Call business contacts.
Connect with members of a professional community.
Set up informational interviews.
Rewrite your resume to match your new idea.
Consult with friends and family.
Clean and organize your home work space for your new activity.
Write an outline for a book, story, or article.
Call an employment agency which specializes in a particular field.
Join a Meetup group.
Go to a networking event.
Contact potential clients.
Do a pro bono project for someone.
Create a new logo or graphical design.
Write down new product names or slogans.
Get a temporary job in your new area of interest.
Register some new internet domain names.

Design a webpage.

Contact someone doing your new activity and request a job shadowing opportunity.

Develop a sales pitch or presentation and practice it with a friend.

Step 4: Integration

Give yourself a few months or more to fully explore all angles of these new opportunities you've identified. If they've led you in a new direction you'd like to pursue, then great! If not, repeat this process starting with the first step, this time adding the new things you've learned from your experiences and removing items which may no longer interest you. Enlist others' help if necessary and repeat this process as needed in order to boost your creative mindset. Keep a simple journal to record your thoughts and feelings on your new activities. You might find that some tasks which make you feel uncomfortable at first become enjoyable as you develop mastery. Take note of your first impressions as well as how you feel later. Allow a few of months of experience to inform your final opinions on any activity you begin.

Day of Kindness

What if you don't have any interests? What if you have no idea what to do or where to start? What if you think, "I'm not interested in anything!" or worse, "I'm not good at anything!"? Both thoughts are false. You may have trouble identifying a specific subject that interests you but you do like to feel good, don't you? Everyone likes to feel good. Personally, I'm interested in anything that makes me feel good. What about you? Does good food make you feel good? Maybe you're interested in food! Does watching TV or movies make you feel good? Maybe you'd like to become a writer! Anything that's a source of pleasure or happiness for you could become a serious interest. But, what if you think you're just not good at anything? If you believe that, you're wrong. There's one thing that everyone is great at, but not everyone practices - kindness. If you're at your wits' end and can't figure out what to do with your life, stop what you're doing, and plan a "day of kindness".

Take your career or vocation off your mind this day. Instead, wake up early and go to as many places around town as you can with the intention of being kind and helpful. To get the most out of it, you'll want to plan this day in advance. Help elderly people cross the street. Help out at a homeless shelter. Find a neighborhood where someone has left a mess and clean it up. Help your neighbor with her yard work. Buy some dog treats and cat food and hand them out to your neighborhood pets. Hang a bird feeder. Hand write a letter to someone who would appreciate a heartfelt thank you. Go try out your favorite jokes in a stand-up comedy routine at an old folks' home. Collect useful household and food items from around your house and donate them to organizations that help the needy. Volunteer to read books to children. Teach children and adult learners to read. Anonymously pay for a stranger's meal or coffee. Don't tell anyone you're doing this unless you intend for them to help you on your day of kindness. Let your creativity be your guide. At the end of the day, take an inventory of how your day of kindness made you feel. Take note of anything special or interesting along the way.

A day of kindness points you in the right direction because being kind has three major effects that can inform your decision-making:

1. It builds empathy. To identify opportunities to practice kindness, you have to look at the world from the perspective of others. You "diagnose" your local community to determine what it needs and how you can help. You anticipate the feelings and needs of others based on their current circumstances. Because each person is unique, members of the same community will diagnose its conditions and identify its needs in different ways. Your community might be geographically local or it might be defined in some other way.

2. It builds creativity. A day of kindness compels you to think about how to solve the problems you've diagnosed. You must determine how your skills can fill those needs and what new skills you may need to learn to make a difference. You might need to recruit other people to help and determine whose skills will best complement your own.

3. It creates a positive feedback loop. You help other people, it makes them and yourself feel good, and those good feelings make you want to help even more. This can help you identify new, more specific ways to take action which are rewarding and fulfilling.

Spending just one day focused solely on your community will go a long way towards making you feel like a valued member of society. It will remind you that everything you do for others really does matter. It will also let the recipients of your kindness know that there are good people in their community who care and that the world is not just a place of greed, hopelessness, pessimism and lack. If you can have such positive effects on people with only one day's work, imagine what you can accomplish throughout an entire career! Your day of kindness will allow you to stop stressing about your career and focus on taking action with a helpful spirit.

Chapter 6 Exercises

Exercise 1. Four-Step Work Identification Process

Follow the four-step process found in this chapter, understanding that it could take several months or more to complete. You may repeat the process multiple times. The key to getting the value from this process is in identifying the takeaways and feedback you receive from each experience and using those to reevaluate your feelings and interests. You'll rule out some areas, investigate new ones, and change others to suit you better.

Exercise 2. Listen To Your Bookshelves

What do your bookshelves say about your interests? Which textbooks have you kept from high school or college? What do you know you should continue learning but you keep putting it off? My bookshelves reflect my interests in foreign languages, metaphysics, computer programming, databases, and statistics. Over 90 percent of the books I own are in these categories. Identify the main themes of the all books you own. What do they reveal about your personal interests? How many of these interests does your current work employ? Think of at least one or two business ideas which involve these topics.

Exercise 3. Childhood Fantasies

Think back to your childhood and recall some of your childhood interests and fantasies. I remember playing by myself in the back yard of my childhood home in Richmond, Virginia where I pretended to teach lessons to imaginary friends. I taught them how to climb a tree and hang on the branches. I also taught them how to stand up and swing on the rope swing my dad had built. I remember setting my stuffed animals all around me in a circle and telling them stories. In my career I've had many opportunities to teach coworkers about database programming and statistics and I've always enjoyed it. Think back to your childhood fantasies. Are there any that you could put to use today?

Exercise 4: What's My Thing?

It often helps to get opinions from people who've had time to form impressions about you. After a while they come to identify certain themes with you and think of you in a specific way. You can gain insight if there is a common theme in the topics with which others associate you. Interview at least one person from each of the following groups: friends, current and former co-workers, and fellow students from a current or past class. Ask them what they think of when they think of you. Do they conjure thoughts of you working on your car in the garage or tending to plants in the garden? Do they consider you the neighborhood computer expert? Are you the person they consider to be an authority on a particular topic? Maybe they associate you with kindness to animals or outdoor adventures. Maybe you were the student who volunteered for a specific project they remember or who always raised his hand to contribute thoughts on a specific topic. It's possible you have preferences and tendencies that many other people recognize but that you take for granted. Identify any trends your interviewees reveal about you. Are these things you take for granted about yourself a potential career pursuit? Of all the things you identify, consider at least one you might like to continue to develop.

Reputation
Ownership
Freedom
Service
Peace
Value
Dominion
Expertise
Independence
Mastery
Community
Philanthropy
leadership
WORK
permits
accounting
marketing
partners
certificates
business plans
financing
networks
legal counselors
ideas
portfolios
artists
schedules
designers

Chapter 7

Take Your Work Seriously

My wife finds it silly when I use sports analogies to describe things that happened at work. I'll use phrases like "down to the wire," "bench strength" and "dropped the ball" without even thinking about it. She's not a sports fan and hasn't worked in business so she doesn't relate. I need to pay more attention to phrases like that which are so ingrained in my vocabulary that I don't notice when they're not appropriate for certain audiences. Sports analogies are so common in business conversations because sports are like a microcosm of the world of business.

My son, who is currently in third grade, plays basketball on his school's team. I started attending his games without any expectations beyond watching him and his schoolmates play. Although I've watched plenty of sports games before, I only recently began to understand what coaches and fans are referring to when they use the word "heart" in reference to a player's performance. I find it amazing that a lot of the players in his games stand around and do little more than watch their teammates and opponents play the game around them. These players seem to be in some zoned out, fugue state of consciousness in which they have no idea that they're actually supposed to be doing something. Anxious cries from coaches and parents fall on their deaf ears. Meanwhile, other players seem like they're fueled with an energized drive to make moves, steal the ball, score, and act with purpose. I've noticed that this drive has nothing to do with the age, sex, or size of the child. One of the best players on his team is a small little girl who dribbles, passes, shoots, steals, and scores. You can tell she's serious by how she plays and by the look on her face. At first, I thought this phenomenon of engaged versus passive players would only apply in children's sports. I assumed all adult professional sports competitors would be fully engaged. To my surprise, I've also noticed vast differences in "heart" in college and professional athletes.

It seems like so many people are doing little more than waiting around every day for someone else to do something that will either improve their lives or make things more interesting. People read the news every day for entertainment and to find out what "important" people are doing. These are the same disengaged people whose only goals in life involve leisure activities. They don't have a strong desire to do anything specific so nothing really changes in their lives. A friend of mine once told me this funny quote, "Most people don't ever do anything because they don't ever *do* anything!" It means that most never achieve because they do not consistently work on anything specific. They aren't working on anything because they don't have any goals that compel them to act.

What are you working on? What's your current plan? What's the reasoning behind it? The answers should be on the tip of your tongue. You should be able to explain it concisely and easily. If it's too complicated sounding, it's likely you haven't defined it well enough. Write it down and read it aloud. Does it make sense? Is it easy to explain? Does it make you feel excited when you read it aloud? If you're still hesitating to begin your productive pursuit, it's likely your perceived obstacles or difficulties outweigh the perceived value of the goal. If this is the case, you need to revisit your goal and determine if it matches your real passions. You can start now. You don't have to wait until your next life just because things aren't "lined up" well enough in this life. If you want something bad enough, almost all constraints can be overcome or avoided in some way. Nothing can stop the truly determined person.

Unsuccessful people know that success in anything worthwhile takes great effort but they're held back by the fear that if they make great efforts and those don't pan out, that they would have wasted their time and energy. They figure that success is relatively unlikely for them so they settle for less. Successful people don't care how much effort it takes to achieve their goal. They don't focus on the effort; they focus on the result. Truly successful people are willing to die trying! This is because whatever they're working on is so important to them that it doesn't matter if they succeed or not. The experiences they gain and the artifacts they produce from their efforts are enough reward and will continue to benefit them in the future.

I've read many books about success, motivation, and successful people and I've come to the conclusion that there is only one difference between people who consider themselves successful and those who do not. Successful people take their pursuits much more seriously than others do. They're constantly developing themselves and their craft. They take consistent daily action toward their goals and align everything in their lives to benefit their primary pursuits. They create businesses around their ideas and hire accountants, lawyers, bankers, publishers, etc. They formalize their ideas with copyrights, licenses, contracts, agreements, vendors, symbols, and logos. They turn their ideas into real-life artifacts and create "somethings" out of seemingly nothing. You don't have to hire all these people up front but you should be thinking of your idea like an ambitious businessperson. Your ideas should have multiple components and phases and you should strategically plan ahead for how you'll carry out each phase of your master plan.

Successful people are often lauded because they "never gave up" or "always persevered." A more accurate and less dramatic way to explain their success is that they "kept trying new things until they found something that worked." They're deeply engrossed in their projects. Their two-step formula is:

1. Keep trying new things over and over until something works.
2. Make sure each new thing is truly interesting and worthwhile for its own sake.

Someone "failing" in a venture is just like a comedian telling a joke that doesn't get laughs. He just goes on to the next joke. Are you merely headed in the direction of your goal or are you really going for it? In this chapter, I encourage you to *operate with a sense of urgency to continually improve yourself and your work.*

Doing Your Duty

Often friends, family, teachers or third parties expect you to follow a particular career path because it's something with which they're familiar and comfortable and can envision you doing. The world at large however, needs you to do more than that. The world needs you to follow a pursuit that gets you to do the unrealistic and the impossible which push forward human progress. Cancer patients, music fans, the environment, and people around the world need you to do more than what is comfortable and easy. My parents knew nothing about computer programming and encouraged me to work in areas they had heard of or could understand. Being a parent myself, I know that parents want to put a cocoon around their children and keep them safe from risk their whole lives. This approach however, doesn't stretch people to develop their full potential and contribute the maximum to society. Some of the most successful people dropped out of college to start their own companies. Their inner calling gave them the courage to follow an unconventional path. It's made a huge difference in my life that I followed my interest in a new field rather than sticking with what was familiar.

The world has an endless desire for new content including new foods, new entertainment, new books, new technology, and new scientific breakthroughs. We need improved ways to manage health, water, energy, computing, medicine, communication, art, information, science and business. Regurgitation of the information written in textbooks only goes so far. We are desperate for ideas and revolutions in all these fields. Nations disagree about issues related to the scarcity of the earth's resources. To the degree that you can make improvements in these areas, you pave the way for improved relations and peace. For this to happen, we need every creative mind working in these fields, including yours.

The possibilities in every field are endless, and the world is incomplete to the extent that you are not developing the area which is most meaningful to you. It's your duty to humanity to develop your ideas and interests to the greatest degree possible. The world is usually willing to pay you for any ideas that interest people. To become successful and help others, you need two things: ideas and audacity. You must begin the soul-searching process by asking yourself what content, desires, and ideas you have that excite and motivate you. This is an iterative process in which you allow yourself to consider anything at all that comes to mind and refine your ideas over and over until you've landed on a specific goal you'd like to achieve. Then you need the audacity to say, "The world needs this, and I'm the person to do it!"

You have unique thoughts, opinions, style, and content that the world needs and can't get anywhere else. Look inside yourself and discover and develop your own new ideas and content. The world needs you to be the best you that you can be. Concentrate hard on developing yourself as much as possible and exchanging value with others in ways that bring the most joy to you and the most value to them. Only you can do your duty because your ideas, talents, and energy are unique. If you don't share your unique value, it will be forever lost to the world.

Professional Portfolio

As you begin to identify the areas of your professional pursuits, you should start developing a professional online portfolio, the content of which will grow and evolve as you progress in your career. If you're in college studying biology for instance, whenever your professors assign you a new project, seriously consider developing a high-quality web version of your project and posting it in your online portfolio. By the time you've graduated from college, you should have an extensive body of work that prospective employers can study before interviewing you, and to which you can refer during interviews.

I've interviewed a few dozen job candidates over the years, and none have referred me to an online portfolio. Several of them however, brought some printed examples of their best work product from previous jobs and it usually was impressive and set them apart from the other candidates. Whether you're applying for a job, doing internet freelancing, or starting your own consulting firm, your online professional portfolio will give prospective employers a great idea of the kind of work you're good at and its level of quality and sophistication.

If I were the president of a university, I would require every student to begin working on a professional online portfolio at the beginning of freshman year. It would be a requirement for graduation that each student present their portfolio to a panel. In typical college courses, professors assign homework and projects for students to complete. The professor grades the students' work, and then it goes in the garbage. Currently, getting a good grade is a student's only motivation to produce a high-quality product. However, if students worked on every project with the intention of adding it to their professional portfolio, they would put more energy into the work because it would represent their best efforts to the outside world. They would do so knowing that they would be referring to it again and again in interviews. Because the content would have future value beyond the classroom, they would take it more seriously. Also, working on a professional portfolio puts students in the mindset and practice of publishing their own content and ideas for which they will eventually start getting paid.

If you're already a working professional, consider resurrecting some of your work on past projects and adding it to a professional portfolio. You likely put a lot of time and effort into it, and could benefit greatly from some residual value in the present. Actors on TV and in movies get paid royalties every time their work is replayed in syndication. You too should get continuing value from your hard work in the past. Graphic artists and web developers usually get permission from clients to display their work in their portfolios to show prospective clients. If your work was on confidential projects for a former employer, you may have to eliminate any confidential items and display your contribution in such a way that the general theme can be understood without compromising any intellectual property.

Having an online professional portfolio shows that you take your work seriously and that you understand the necessity of communicating its value to others. When applying for jobs or other business opportunities, a typical resume, no matter how well written, may not be enough to propel you to the top of the stack. Having a serious online professional portfolio will immediately differentiate you from those who don't have one. My professional portfolio can be found at www.distinctanalytics.com. I've referred to it countless times during telephone and in-person interviews with hiring managers and recruiters. It has always impressed my audience, as much because I was the only candidate who had one as because of the content. If at any point you're feeling gloomy about your career prospects, add more content to your professional portfolio to strengthen your brand and brighten your spirits. If you take away only one thing from this book, let it be this.

Goal Setting

Once you've done the hard work of identifying your interests, it's time to set goals and work towards them. Everything I've ever read about goal setting stresses the importance of writing down your goals. That's because it works! It actually worked for me when I was studying for the CPA exam. Months before the exam, I took a helpful exam review course and prepared the traditional way using huge, intimidating study books. The exam took place over two days with two four-hour parts each day separated by a lunch break. It was quite difficult and required recalling a lot of information as well as having the stamina to sit through two four-hour sessions per day. I failed the exam the first time I took it and began to look for better ideas on how to approach the process.

I had heard about writing down your goals, so I got a piece of paper and started to write a goal about passing the CPA exam. I thought it would be a simple exercise to write one or two sentences and then put the paper away somewhere. As I started to put pen to paper, I immediately felt a wave of anxiety rush over me. I realized that I couldn't just write it down without committing myself emotionally to the goal. I felt like writing it down would make the goal more real and the personal failure greater if I wasn't able to pass the exam. I felt like I was setting myself up to be a poser, the way I had felt as a child when I had climbed the ladder to the top of the high diving board at the pool, walked to the end of the board, but had to walk back and climb down because I was too afraid to jump.

I went ahead and wrote down the goal anyway but determined to figure out a new way to study that would improve my results from the previous time and do justice to my new commitment. I wanted to study hard and smart enough so that if I didn't pass, at least I would know that I gave my best effort possible and feel satisfied with that. I felt that if I properly developed and executed a good plan, that would be a good enough achievement to allow me to put this issue to rest one way or the other. I remembered that the exam review professor had given us students a computer study course on a series of floppy disks. From the shed in the backyard, I dug up the old computer my parents had bought me when I was in high school, and it worked with the floppy disk program. There were 3,000 multiple choice questions on the disks so I divided that by the number of days until the exam and determined that I had to complete 55 questions each day. I took notes on the questions I missed in four notebooks (one for each part of the exam) and spent the last two weeks before the exam studying those notebooks. On the second sitting, I passed all four parts of the exam, earning the lowest possible passing score on each part. However, I was thrilled and amazed to have passed considering my college grades in accounting weren't very good. I earned the dubious distinction of joining the informal "300 Club", because the lowest passing score on each of the four parts was 75. My parents had given me a hard time about my low grades in accounting in college, so at dinner on the night I received my results, I brought up the subject of my poor grades. I said something like, "Remember how we've talked about my having a low GPA in college? Let's forget about 'GPA' and let's talk about 'CPA'!" The feeling was incredible.

I suggest you research the concept of "SMART" goals and structure your goals that way. Keep your written goals in a place where you will see them regularly. If you can't avoid seeing them, you'll be faced with the decision of either achieving the goals or erasing them if you've decided they no longer apply. Hopefully you'll replace them with better goals and continue thinking about how you can squeeze in some extra time somewhere in your schedule to work on them. My wallet has one of those flaps with a clear window so you can see what's inside. That's where I put a piece of paper or card with some short or medium-term goals written down. When I've completed one of them, I'll either mark it off or replace it with new piece of paper with my updated goals rewritten. In addition to or in place of your written goal, you can use a picture or symbol as a visible goal reminder.

Develop your favorite way to structure your written goals. One way is to have your major goals, like "write a mystery novel" or "open an ice cream shop" or "get hired at Company X" written as headings. Under each heading, write down the steps you're going to take this week as subheadings. When you complete each step, cross it off the list. Crossing off items feels great and gives you more motivation to work on the next item and cross that off.

Some people working towards a goal equate their distance from the goal with their degree of satisfaction. In other words, the further they are from the goal, the less content they are with the process. This way of thinking makes loftier goals more difficult because they take longer to achieve and involve more doubt in the meantime. The real meat of achieving a goal is taking small consistent steps in the right direction. The discipline to consistently take those steps makes you as successful now as you will be when you achieve your goal. This is because "getting" is just a byproduct of "doing". If you focus on the "doing", the results will take care of themselves. If you've identified a goal for yourself, make a plan for the specific steps you'll take to chip away at it. Then, de-emphasize the goal and focus instead on how you'll regularly address the steps in your plan. If you can make the steps a habit you would repeat even if you never ended up achieving the goal, then you'll have already succeeded.

Don't underestimate the power of writing down goals. If you don't have any goals written down, are you sure you're really moving towards something specific or are you just floating around? If I ever meet you in person, I'd like to think you might pull out your wallet and show me your written goals. I don't need to see what they are specifically, just that you have something written down.

Chapter 7 Exercises

Exercise 1: What are you coming out with?

A large multimedia entertainment company recently announced that in the next few years it is coming out with sixteen new popular fantasy movies. This huge effort will cost hundreds of millions of dollars, and involve thousands of people in supreme coordination. The company's management has developed elaborate documented strategies and plans covering every detail of these ventures. When these movies come out, they will likely be very entertaining, popular and profitable.

What are you coming out with? What plans, developments, and strategies are you working on? Are you opening a new coffee house? Are you working on a book? Developing a website? Are you adding to your creative portfolio? Specifically, what content you are working on right now that can be shared with other people? Examples of content include a recipe, a website, a mobile app, a book, a play, a poem, a schematic drawing of a new system for something, a computer program, a catalog of something, or a product you can offer. Are you curating other content in a way that will make it easier for people to consume? If you're not currently "coming out with" anything right now, consider ways you could become a producer of some kind of content that could be consumed by other people or businesses. Think of things you could produce or publish that could help other people in some way and result in some sort of financial return for you.

Exercise 2: Online Professional Portfolio

If you had an online portfolio as described in this chapter, what would it look like? How many pages would your website have and what topics would it cover? How would it represent your personal style? Creating a professional portfolio forces you to define a descriptive vision of your skillset and offerings. Getting your ideas out of your mind and onto paper in a specific incarnation allows you to think more critically about them and exposes them to the (usually) helpful scrutiny of other people. I once created a website on which I intended to host both my personal information (favorite movies, jokes, links, recipes, etc.) and my professional portfolio. Once it was complete, I received feedback from my friends who told me it might be wiser to keep personal and professional areas separate. I then realized my site was pretty cheesy and that I needed to start over. This led to creating one site for my business intelligence work (www.distinctanalytics.com), another for career coaching (www.uniquecareerpath.com), and scrapping the idea of having a personal website. This made the most sense to me only after exposing my original ideas to opportunities for refinement.

You don't need to know how to program websites in order to create an online portfolio. Get some markers and several pieces of paper and draw a rough sketch of what your website would look like. One piece of paper could be the home page and others could be linked pages with different types of content on them. View other online portfolios for ideas. If you don't want to do any programming, you can develop your whole portfolio on paper and pay a web developer to create the site for you. Also, there are many free online portfolio-hosting websites and web development tools you can use. Your first efforts may not be your best but you have to start somewhere in order to begin the iterative improvement process.

Exercise 3: Written Goals

Do you have a wallet, purse, or bathroom mirror you could use for displaying written goals? On an index card or small piece of paper, write down one or two goals as headings and, underneath each heading, write small achievable steps you can take in the short term. Keep the written goals someplace you'll see them often and be forced to regularly consider when you'll work on the items under the headings. Over time, as you see the written goals regularly, you'll also consider whether or not they continue to resonate with you and whether you should reevaluate them. Cross off items you've completed and add new ones that follow. Ask friends, colleagues and mentors about their experiences writing down goals.

Conclusion

As you achieve success in your career, it's important to keep in mind a pitfall that occurs in proportion to the size of the success. When you succeed at something, you immediately begin to associate yourself with that thing. Your success serves as "proof" that what you succeeded in is the right thing for you. Lazy thinking reinforces this by making you think you've finally found your "life's calling". There's no such thing as a "life's calling" just like there's no such thing as a "soulmate." You can succeed in many vocations and get along well with many life partners. You're just as multi-dimensional a person as you were before your success in a specific area. Typecasting yourself will only serve to limit the increased options your success just delivered to you. You were not "meant" to do anything specific and you don't have any "special affinity" for anything. Any above-average skills you may have, say, in math, music or languages, should increase, not decrease your options. The only thing your success proves is your ability to produce good results. After how hard you've worked to succeed, you should have more options, not fewer. Don't let success (or anything else for that matter) define who you are or what you can do.

Remember yourself at ten years old. You thought you'd never grow up, that you had all the time in the world - too much time in fact. You certainly knew less about the world than you do now. What hopes and dreams did you have then? What did you want to be when you grew up? Did you think big thoughts and entertain impossible ideas? Take a moment to consider your life as it is today. Have you done justice to that child's expectations? Would she be afraid or disappointed to learn what her future has become? Or would she be proud to become the person you are today? If you haven't done well by that child, there's still time.

Innumerable opportunities and hidden avenues exist towards almost any wants, needs, or goals you may have. Only your personal misconceptions about yourself and the world hold you back. What you want is not as far-fetched as you think. You may be closer to getting it than you realize. Opportunities are not as limited as you think. Success is in great supply! Every obstacle to what you want in your life is loaded with cracks, fissures, and holes. In case you don't have the good fortune to walk through the front door of the opportunity you desire, you must realize that there are endless side and back doors. As soon as you accept that this is true, your perceived limitations will begin to fade away. I sincerely hope the material in this book has helped you envision your career in more creative and productive ways.

Career Principles

1. Make your career goal something specific other than money.

2. Measure your achievement based solely on the amount of value you provide for other people.

3. Make sure your education provides you with lots of valuable skills and options.

4. Identify and perfect your personal style to gain confidence in yourself and your potential.

5. Optimize every area of your life to support your goals.

6. Develop and refine your interests through exposure, experience, and trial and error.

7. Operate with a sense of urgency to continually improve yourself and your work.

Contributor Acknowledgement

This book has benefitted immeasurably from these contributors, all local Las Vegas entrepreneurs, to whom I owe a debt of gratitude. Both their creativity and scrutiny have added value that I couldn't have on my own.

Meegan Boiros
www.meeganboirosfineart.com

Meegan painted the painting which became the cover art for the book. A professional oil painter for over 25 years, most of her work consists of commissions. She brought my art concept to life through her unique style and talent.

Brian T. Cox
www.briantcox.com

Brian created the graphic illustrations at the beginning of each chapter. As well as being a talented professional artist, Brian also excels in music, photography, video, woodworking, and graphic design. He dramatically improved upon my original art concepts and was never satisfied until he'd hit a home run with each piece.

Tiffany King
www.tiffanysedits.com

Tiffany edited the manuscript and provided copy and content advice. Her experience as a professional editor and writer and her passion for inspirational content were exactly what the project needed. She transformed the manuscript from clumsy to concise.

Made in United States
Orlando, FL
08 January 2023